Believe That I Am Here

Believe That I Am Here

The Notebooks
of Nicole Gausseron
BOOK ONE

Translated from the French by
William Skudlarek, O.S.B. and Hilary Thimmesh, O.S.B.

LOYOLAPRESS.

CHICAGO

LOYOLAPRESS.

3441 N. ASHLAND AVENUE
CHICAGO, ILLINOIS 60657
(800) 621-1008
WWW.LOYOLABOOKS.ORG

This book, published in three volumes, is a revised, re-edited, and sub-stantially expanded version of *The Little Notebook,* originally pub-lished as one volume in 1996 in the United States by HarperCollins.

All Scripture quotations are from the New Revised Standard Version Bible: Catholic Edition, copyright © 1993 and 1989 by the Division of Christian Education of the National Council of the Churches of Christ in the U.S.A. Used by permission. All rights reserved.

Cover and interior design by Judine O'Shea
Cover photo: Mel Curtis/Photonica

Library of Congress Cataloging-in-Publication Data

Gausseron, Nicole.
  Believe that I am here : the notebooks of Nicole Gausseron /
translated from the French by William Skudlarek and Hilary
Thimmesh.
      p. cm.
Rev. ed. of: The little notebook.
  ISBN 0-8294-1621-8
 1. Gausseron, Nicole--Diaries. 2. Catholics--France--Diaries. 3.
Visions. 4. Jesus Christ--Apparitions and miracles--France--Chartres.
5. Compagnons du Partage. 6. Church work with the homeless--
France--Chartres. 7. Chartres (France)--Church history--20th
century. I. Gausseron, Nicole. Little notebook. II. Title.
  BX4705.G2636A3 2003
  282'.092--dc21

                                        2003012152

Printed in the United States of America
   04 05 06 07 08 09 10 M-V 10 9 8 7 6 5 4 3 2

A cross the green fields of the Beauce, the rich wheat-growing region of France southwest of Paris, the famous silhouette of the cathedral of Notre-Dame de Chartres has beckoned to pilgrims for eight hundred years. Americans are likely to identify Chartres with the cathedral. To the people who live there, however, the city is not only the site of that great medieval structure but also a bustling regional center with typical modern economic and social problems, among them the needs of the poor.

Concern for the poor, particularly the homeless men who survive somehow on the fringes of society, led a woman of Chartres to help establish and to become the first director of a home for such men in 1981. She called it the *Compagnons du Partage,* a phrase not very satisfactorily translated as "Companions in Sharing." She started on a shoestring, aided by Bernard Dandrel—who would later found the first European Food Bank—and the first year in particular was touch and go.

The woman's name is Nicole. She comes from a distinguished family and is well educated. In fact she holds a degree in British literature and taught for a time before her marriage to Philippe Gausseron. They both possessed that mix of intelligence and style that one thinks of as characteristically French: understated, responsible, serious, but also attuned to warm friendship and the joy of living.

At the time that Nicole started her home for homeless men she was in her late thirties, and she and Philippe had three children—Laurette, Benoît, Thierry—ages seven to eleven. She had recently had the charismatic experience of baptism in the Holy Spirit, and she had come to know the poor through volunteer service with *Secours Catholique,* a national charitable organization of the French Catholic Church, of which Philippe was for ten years the local president.

Some of the poor, she discovered, needed not only a meal but a place to live and work, at least for a time. She set about providing such a place. The mayor of Chartres made an unused barracks on the edge of town available rent-free. Friends and well-wishers contributed odds and ends of furniture. The first day the doors were open, three men moved in; the second day, seven more. The *Compagnons du Partage* was off to a shaky start and depended on Nicole's constant attention to keep going.

The story of the *Compagnons du Partage* is more complicated than that, of course, but it is only partly the story of *The Notebooks of Nicole Gausseron,* which begins about four years after the founding of the Companions and transforms Nicole's experience into a universal and timeless story. Struggling to care for her two communities, as she calls them—her family and the men who came to live at the Companions—and always with inadequate resources, she was on the brink of abandoning her efforts after nine months of struggle when Pierre Maghin came to live with the Companions. Pierre was a priest of the Archdiocese of Paris who, with his bishop's blessing, had become a worker-priest in the late sixties. Bernard Dandrel had met him at a charismatic prayer meeting in Chartres and had approached him about becoming the director of the Community. On the day that he reserved the Sacrament in a makeshift chapel, Nicole knew the *Compagnons du Partage* would continue. It was for her the beginning of a new relationship with Jesus. In the celebration of the Eucharist in this modest setting, Jesus revealed his presence as a living person with feelings of his own, a friend sharing her burdens and her joys, the Lord speaking to her and to others through her about their indispensable part in his kingdom.

The Notebooks of Nicole Gausseron is a record of her encounters with Jesus, kept day by day in her *petit cahier,* her little notebook. The *Notebooks,* which are published in three volumes in this English edition, cover twelve years in

Nicole's life, from the mid-1980s to the late 1990s. The outward events of those years are lively, as the notebooks reveal—during that time Nicole raised a family while engaging in a demanding ministry to homeless men. We read of many joys—and a full measure of sorrow—in her life. But of even greater interest is the record Nicole kept of her inner life—especially the unfolding of her relationship with her friend Jesus.

A few words about how to read the *Notebooks* may be helpful. They are first of all virtually devoid of the reverential tone that we are accustomed to in works of piety. The style is much more like that of the Gospel accounts of Jesus' ministry—episodic, terse, objective. Continuity results from the development of central themes rather than sustained narrative. This method is incremental. It builds to something of great substance and consistency, but the reader can only know that—as Nicole came to know it—by starting with slight and fragmentary impressions.

Impressions is a key word. Nicole is not a visionary. In one of her first entries in the *Notebooks* she observes that the Lord is "seated beside us" but that "It's not a shadow or an apparition, but a presence." She often gives this presence a visual form and a location but never a detailed description.

The *Notebooks* present neither visions nor special revelations. Quite the contrary, Nicole earns a firm rebuff whenever she pushes the boundary of divine omniscience. "Is there a hell?" she asks, and Jesus replies, "Why are you so concerned about my Father's affairs?" She would like to know what will become of some unfortunate men, and Jesus tells her, "Do not try to know everything." This steadfast refusal to traffic in inside information about the spiritual realm, to claim privileged insights or private revelations, is to our mind one of the strongest arguments for the authenticity of these journals. The words of Jesus that Nicole reports tell us no more than the Gospels tell us.

The value of the *Notebooks* lies in their cogent reminder of how much the Gospels do tell us about Jesus—and about ourselves in relation to him. There is nothing imaginary or remote about the Jesus who speaks to Nicole, smiles at her, is amused by her recollection of a refrain from an old love song, shows just a hint of weariness in reassuring her of his love for the umpteenth time, and once, to her astonishment, admits to a touch of jealousy. If the risk for believers is to relegate Jesus to resplendent glory as the *Kyrios,* the glorified Lord who is infinitely remote from daily life and correspondingly irrelevant, the Jesus who speaks in these pages insists on avoiding that risk by being one of us here and now. The bedrock reality is that he lives now and seeks a personal relationship with those who believe in him. This assurance is repeated and emphasized. "I am not an abstract idea or a system, but a living person." Nicole's repeated expression of concern for others occasions what is perhaps the most surprising theme in the *Notebooks,* one that may jar readers accustomed to easy pieties about serving God in one another. Jesus teaches Nicole that she must first of all respond directly to his love, attend to him, recognize his priority. She is free, as are all, to respond to him or not. He will not bind her; you don't bind those you love, and besides, he and his Father "have no need for puppets." But if she responds to his love, she must not forget him in her concern for others. In the end she can do nothing for others that he doesn't do through her, and he is also in those others, even the alcoholics who leave the *Compagnons du Partage* to all appearances no better off than when they came. Her responsibility and what she can do for others are limited; her relationship to Jesus is unlimited.

As Nicole continues to direct the *Compagnons du Partage* and to befriend the homeless and broken men who come to live and work together on the outskirts of Chartres, they, in turn, continue to reveal to her not only a Jesus who shares in the sufferings of this world but also a Jesus who loves her and all people with a love that is unconditional and unbounded.

One of the most important features of this remarkable journal is its implicit claim that a deeply personal and experiential knowledge of God goes hand in hand with deeply personal and experiential service to the poor. That claim is, of course, right at the heart of the New Testament: "How does God's love abide in anyone who has the world's goods and sees a brother or sister in need and yet refuses help?" (1 John 3:17). It is not uncommon, however, to find Christians—today as well as in times past—dividing themselves into opposing camps: those who claim to be true disciples of Jesus because they devote themselves to the spiritual life, and those who claim to be his true followers because they work for social justice. Nicole's experience of an intensely personal relationship with Jesus is grounded in her direct and loving contact with people who smell bad, who cheat, lie, and steal—even from her—and is thereby rendered all the more authentic.

Finally, a word should be said about the distinctly Catholic tone of this journal. Many, perhaps even most of, Nicole's dialogues with Jesus occur at Mass, usually in the Chapel of the Companions, where Pierre celebrates daily. Nicole often spends a half-hour in prayer before the Blessed Sacrament.

Belief in the real presence of Jesus in the sacrament of the Eucharist and the act of remaining before it in an attitude of adoration provide Nicole with a way of focusing her attention and prayer. But it should also be noted that Nicole's practice of gazing at the consecrated Communion wafer is more than just a method or technique for entering into a contemplative style of prayer. What it offers is a way of prolonging the act of praise and thanksgiving that is central to eucharistic worship and to the Christian life. Often she complains that it is hard to turn to praise in the midst of so much suffering. Patiently and lovingly, Jesus shows her that praise and thanksgiving are not ultimately to be located in feelings of well-being or in understanding why things are as they are but in maintaining a heart-to-heart relationship with him in spite of, and in the midst of, suffering.

Nicole's sense of the immediate presence of Jesus during the eucharistic celebration is rooted in and shaped by the Scriptures. On numerous occasions the dialogue between Nicole and Jesus is directly related to the scriptural passages that are read and meditated on in the celebration of the Eucharist. As one might guess from reading the *Notebooks,* the style of the celebration of the Eucharist in the Chapel of the Companions is quite different from the "oh-so-traditional" Sunday liturgies in her parish church.

At the Community the pace is more relaxed, and there is ample opportunity for personal and spontaneous prayer. Nicole's words to Jesus are sometimes spoken aloud during these pauses for personal prayer, and on occasion Jesus asks her to convey his words to the small congregation that has come together for worship.

It may be helpful to note that the men who seek shelter at the *Compagnons du Partage* are welcomed in the name of Jesus but are not obliged to participate in any religious activities. The only conditions for living in the Community are that they not use drugs or alcohol and that they be willing to contribute to the work of the Community during their stay, which for most is a period of about three months. The work consists of collecting and repairing used goods and selling them in a secondhand store.

The Hermitage to which Nicole often refers is a farm about five miles from Chartres acquired in 1985 to provide more adequate living quarters for the Companions. The administrative center and place of work on the outskirts of the city is consistently referred to as the Community, and *Companion* is capitalized when it refers to a resident of the *Compagnons du Partage.*

In our judgment this remarkable journal modestly makes an extraordinary claim: that the Jesus of faith has given this teaching about himself to a woman of Chartres in our time. We have found that *The Notebooks of Nicole Gausseron* reveal their depths on repeated reading. Read straight through, the *Notebooks* give readers a sense of the movement of the journey that Jesus asks his followers to embark on, but each volume also rewards the random reader. On almost every page there is a word or statement that helps one understand more clearly and more concretely that a deep and personal relationship with Jesus—and, through Jesus, with God—is the heart and soul of the Christian life and that it contributes to the "weaving of the kingdom" when it is given expression in a preferential love for the poor.

William Skudlarek, O.S.B.
Hilary Thimmesh, O.S.B.

Saint John's Abbey, Collegeville, Minnesota

March 22

The Beauce isn't really flat. That's what I'm thinking about on my way to see my friend Anna, who has just lost her husband, 54, to lung cancer. It was only last night that the three of us spent an hour and a half together at the hospital.

Anna asked me to pray for him. The only words that came to my lips were "Mary . . . Mary . . . Jesus . . . Jesus . . . ," and then all by myself I labored through the Our Father and the Hail Mary. Silently I begged, "Lord, take him soon. Come for him. He's ready. Take him." In my anguish I cried out, "Hurry up, Lord! What are you waiting for?"

Yes, I dared to ask him what he was waiting for! And now in the car driving back to see Anna again I dare to speak to him:

> Lord, what am I going to say? How can I console her?
>
> ✝ *Do not search for words, Nicole. Do not prepare anything.*
>
> Lord, it's hard for her. It's just awful.
>
> ✝ *Yes, I know, Nicole. I know.*

The road runs on. Silence sets in. The sight of the snow on the fields is lovely and soothing. I start to cry.

> ✝ *Nicole, why do you blame me? You are asking me to render an account. Nicole, Nicole . . .*

Lord, it's hard to follow you. I don't know where I'm going.

I weep. My tears flow abundantly. There are only the two of us so I don't care. I'm not ashamed of crying. This is my way of speaking to him, too.

> ✝ *Nicole, look at the road off in the distance.*

I'm looking, Lord.

> ✝ *Can you make it out?*

No.

> ✝ *And now?*

Yes, Lord, now I can see it.

(Didn't I say that the Beauce isn't flat!)

> ✝ *Nicole, just now you did not see it and yet it was there. Do not worry about your road.*

But, Lord, I'm frightened when I don't know where I'm going. I like to see the road ahead of me. I need to see it.

> ✝ *Nicole, have I ever abandoned you? Give me one example.*

I don't have any examples for you. I'm thinking,
but there aren't any.

✢ *Well then?*

That's where we stopped. I didn't cry anymore. I felt his
sorrow, not mine.

When I saw my friend and her five children, I didn't
bother trying to come up with anything. We talked and
prepared the petitions for Mass. During lunch we lis-
tened to each other. It was simple, warm, moving. You
were there, Lord.

Now and then I'm affected by a kind of vertigo. It will soon
be four years that I have been involved with a community
of twenty men. That's where my energies are spent.
Physically, morally, and psychologically the Companions
are my second family. If you want to help the down-and-
out, you have to go beyond words and pious sentiments.
There can be no limits on your love. You have to let listening, patience, and sensitivity take over your life. It's a road
without end. You muddle through with what you've got at
hand, with how things look today, and with what your own
heart tells you. It's all-absorbing and emotionally draining,
even if I'm not at it twenty-four hours a day.

Yes, a kind of vertigo comes over me every so often. A little
voice says, "What's the use? Why go through so much
trouble for a handful of men?" Or again, "Ten years of
study to become a prof. You were good at teaching. Why
put yourself out for a few good-for-nothings?"

This little voice full of reason and good sense leaves me confused. And then the other day on my way to the Community, the answer came, plain and simple. It was the image of a worn garment, threadbare, coming apart at the seams. This garment is the Companion who comes knocking at our door. The Lord needs us to patch up this garment with what we've got at hand, not to make a new one. We are only responsible for the sewing, the mending we try to do. If the garment tears apart anyway, that doesn't depend on us, or on me personally.

March 27

Often during the Eucharist and especially after the Consecration, I have an almost physical sense of the presence of Christ. Standing or seated, his hands often extended, he invades me with his presence. I'm overwhelmed by a feeling of tenderness and simplicity.

I feel so protected at those moments that a strange numbness comes over me. I lose all sense of space and time. The people next to me are at once far away, and yet very close. The experience is measureless, but at the same time very simple. I shed tears of joy as I speak to him.

> Lord, I'm a little scared. Am I losing my mind?
> Why are you giving me all this? If it is you,
> you're pampering me too much.
>
> ✝ *I have chosen you because I love you.*
>
> Lord, why me? Look at me. I'm not worthy. You
> know very well that I don't put you in first place
> all the time.
>
> ✝ *Because I need you, Nicole, just as you are.*

The tone of his response seems to betray a certain weariness, as if he were repeating the same words for the nth time. To him it seems so obvious and simple. I discover at that instant, or rather I realize again, that I am a sinner, but not in a negative sense. Rather it's a lack of something, a lack of giving or of receiving. Experiencing the tenderness of Jesus immerses you. You want to give back, to respond with thanks for this gift, and you realize how poor you are.

March

On several occasions, now, the Lord has been seated beside us. After the Consecration he's here. It's not a shadow or an apparition, but a presence. Once at the Carmel, several times at the chapel: he's here, seated, silent.

> Why are you sitting here, Lord? You're silent.
> You're not saying anything.

✝ *I am here.*

> You must have something to say to us, to tell
> me. It's a bit disconcerting to have you so close.
> You put me at ease. I do feel a certain serenity
> knowing you're here, but I don't understand
> what you're trying to tell me.

No answer. Silence filled with his presence. Pierre prays in tongues. The answer springs to my lips.

✝ *Nourish yourselves with my Eucharist.*

> In other words, Lord, you simply want me to
> take advantage of you?

✝ *Yes.*

> But that's so simple, Lord; it's almost easy.

✝ *Yes, it is.*

His presence fills me. Once more I lose all sense of space and time. Around me it's as if everything were stretching away. At one and the same time I'm firmly seated on my shabby little tabouret and somewhere else . . . at one with him. It's nothing sensational. I feel perfectly calm.

Lord, you don't say much; you're not much of a talker.

✝ *No, I am not.*

Pardon me for being so insistent, Lord, but I'd like to get this into my head.

Silence again. I have the impression of butting up against him, and his silence intrigues me. For my part I try to empty myself, to be completely new so as to get a better grasp of what his presence says to us. Gradually the meaning dawns on me.

Lord, you are what for us is inaccessible, foolish, impossible. Is that it?

✝ *Yes.*

Everything comes together in you, Lord. It's useless to look elsewhere. Is that it, Lord?

✝ *Yes.*

April 19

The Lord is once more seated beside me. A silent and comforting presence.

> Lord, you immerse us in your love. It's too much, almost too beautiful.

> ✝ *It is free, Nicole . . . It is easy. I have already told you. Be like a wisp of straw; let go.*

> Why, Lord? Do you want to reassure me in the face of trials to come? Do you want to help me ahead of time?

> ✝ *No, it is free.*

> As if you wish to reassure me about what might happen.

> ✝ *I take the lead.*

April 22

An old pig barn. The Companions have just cleaned it up. It's simple, empty, but still a little grimy. We were thinking about making it into a chapel.

Today I ask him:

> Lord, do you want it to be a chapel?
>
> ✝ *Yes.*
>
> It's quite empty and bare.
>
> ✝ *It is like me, Nicole.*
>
> Then we'll do it, Lord.

I had gone there weighed down by the events of the day, but suddenly I felt restored. Getting into the truck that takes us back to Chartres, one of the Companions says to me:

"There's something funny about the way you look. You seem to be somewhere else."

"Yes, Patrick, I am kind of somewhere else."

After the Eucharist this evening the tenderness of God enfolds me. I'd like to stretch out on the rug, I feel so relaxed. My body is almost asleep, but not my soul.

I question him:

> Lord, you see our day. The people we've dealt with. It's heavy-going.

> ✝ *Yes.*

> Following you is rather heavy-going. You charge a pretty high price. We continually have to listen, be patient, urge one, comfort another . . .

> ✝ *But Nicole, I am not expensive. I am always here. Come. Come and visit me. Take me. You can do that anytime.*

> Okay, I understand, but it's not restful or reassuring.

> ✝ *I do not offer a superhighway. This is another kind of road. It climbs, it drops, it turns . . .*

And then in the silence, as if he were a little ashamed to put the question to me for the nth time, he asks me once more with the modesty of those who truly love:

> ✝ *Do you want to follow me?*

April 23

The Lord comes toward us. He is carrying a bundle in his arms. Maybe a child?

What are you carrying, Lord?

✛ *You and the Companions.*

Why are you doing that?

✛ *To help you when things are too hard.*

Do you do this often?

✛ *Every time you need it. When the road is easier, when it gives you less trouble, I let you walk.*

April 25

I walk to the Community along this grim, colorless street. To me this long row of gray houses and that endless military building with its empty windows seem to have no soul.

My heart sinks as I pass a disreputable bar for the umpteenth time.

Male or female, young or old, it's a weird menagerie whose path I cross.

> Lord, take a look at your humanity. It's pretty sad.

Silence.

> Don't you feel like talking, Lord?

> ✝ *I did not spend my whole life talking, you know.*

> True, Lord. Do you have something to say to me?

> ✝ *Yes. Be.*

> . . .

✝ *Live. Be. Be yourself. Draw life from me. Let me speak and live in you.*

And in the evening, in the chapel:

Lord, you're very quiet.

✝ *Yes.*

Why?

✝ *I have already spoken to you quite often.*

And so?

✝ *Meditate on what I have said to you. Internalize it.*

April 26

✣ *Give me the whole place.*

Lord, I thought that's what we were doing.
Don't you feel at ease?

✣ *I need room among you.*

Do you find things a little cramped here?

✣ *My spirit goes everywhere, as it will, where it will. Let it be free. Give it plenty of room.*

April 30

This evening an image of a deep torrent of water—violent, laden with debris. A huge black rock juts out from the riverbank. Branches and twigs bump against it, lodge in its cracks, then whirl away again in the current.

May

I pass by a halfway house for men released from prison. Everything is clean, the lawns raked, the flower beds blooming, the rooms tidy. And yet I know that the men there find the place stifling. They prefer the Community, even though the barracks we use are really ugly, our courtyard littered with paper, everything so dull and gray.

> Lord, do you see these wretched people in their gilded prison?
>
> ✝ *Yes.*
>
> They need something more than cleanliness and right-angled walks. What they lack is love.
>
> ✝ *Yes, I know.*
>
> Lord, what needs to be done?
>
> ✝ *Pray. Ask me.*

May

After the Eucharist.

> Lord, yesterday you told us to ask. I ask that
> your will be done, but send harvesters for the
> poor, Lord. Look how they cry out to you.

> ✝ *And I, I ask you this, Nicole: Do you believe I*
> *can do that?*

> Yes . . . Yes . . . You can.

> ✝ *Well then, if you really believe it, I will do it. I*
> *need the faith of all of you. I need you to want*
> *it with your whole being, to really believe I*
> *can do it.*

> Yes, Lord, we believe you can.

> ✝ *Do you accept not knowing where you are,*
> *being confused by my paths, my way of*
> *doing things?*

> Yes, Lord.

My *yes* is a little timid.

May 6

It's my birthday today, Lord. It doesn't look as if anybody has remembered.

Silence.

I was hoping for a party. You know how important that is to me. But the thought hasn't even occurred to them. You'd think I didn't have anything to do with them.

✝ *No, you belong to me.*

May 7

Lord, it's difficult to be like a child before you.

✢ *They have not only disfigured my face and my body. They have also distorted my words.*

What do you mean, Lord?

✢ *To be a child is to let me live in you. To permit me to dwell in you, to act in you. It is enough to say yes to me, and I will come and love in you.*

May 8

Lord, tell me why so many people go right by you without recognizing you, even though they're looking for you.

✝ *They are looking for the wrong thing.*

The wrong thing?

✝ *They want an answer, a formula. But I have nothing to offer but myself, and that means a way of life.*

What is this way of life?

✝ *To live with me, day after day, hour after hour.*

May 9

It's hard to pray to you. When I come before you, I feel scattered.

✝ *I am the one who draws things together, who centers.*

I feel empty, not up to it.

✝ *I love all of you as you are at this moment. My love accepts you as you are. My love is simple.*

May 10

The Gospel of John: "I have called you friends."

Lord, you change our status from servants to friends. Does that mean we can ask you for anything we want?

✝ *No.*

Look at the world. See how bad things are.

✝ *You do not know how to look.*

May 12

Text of St. Paul, 1 Corinthians 13:7: Love "bears all things."

Lord, this *all* bothers me. Surely you can see
that people don't do what St. Paul says. Even
two people who love each other.

✝ *You have not understood it at all.*

Well then, explain it to me.

✝ *With me you can get to the* all. *It is true; in
many ways you fall short, but I supply what is
missing. I make up for your deficiencies. I
come to the rescue if you ask me.*

May 14

Lord, what a poor tortured king you make upon the cross.

✝ *Why "poor"?*

. . . ?

✝ *My body, my blood, these are the symbols of my royalty. No one can take these from me. I have given them freely.*

May 16

✝ *Do not weigh yourself down with useless burdens.*

What burdens, Lord?

✝ *Life, the destiny of others, yesterday, tomorrow.*

Then what are we to do?

✝ *Live this moment. I am giving it to you. It is my gift. Do not let yourself be preoccupied with what may be in the future.*

May 17

✝ *I call you my friends. You are tied to me by a string, a thin thread, almost invisible.*

Why not a rope, Lord?

✝ *Because then you would pay attention to the rope and not to me. And besides, you do not bind those you love.*

May 18

"Ask and you will receive, so that your joy may be complete" (the Gospel of John 16:24). This isn't a place I'm used to, this remote little chapel with its community of sisters in gray and red habits. I feel a twinge of pain in my heart at the beginning of Mass because I'm afraid that the Lord will not speak to me.

He enters and remains standing at the back of the church.

> Lord, thank you for coming here, for being for us and with us.

Silence.

> Lord, aren't you going to come forward and take a seat near the altar? Why do you remain standing at the back of this tiny chapel?

> ✝ *Look, the essential is in front of you, my body and my blood. That is the way it should be. No one can distort anything.*

And then a few moments later:

> ✝ *Do not be afraid. I will not abandon you.*

I need to feel you.

> ✝ *Ask. Ask not to be afraid anymore.*

May 19

The little gray and red sisters are all smiles as they welcome us. From the very beginning of Mass a sort of communion is established among us. The Lord comes to take a seat near the altar. He's dressed in white and he smiles happily.

Lord, are you taking your place up front today?

✝ *Yes.*

But why is that?

No answer. I realize that he's there just the same—seated, still, peaceful. I don't understand until after the reading of John, chapter 17.

Is it to show us your Father, to send us to him?

✝ *Yes.*

Lord, here I am crying again. Do you know why?

✝ *Yes.*

You speak to me in the same way you and the Father speak to each other. I am overwhelmed.

✝ *Yes.*

You use the same language. It's powerful even
though it's wordless.

I don't ask him anything else. I try to be as prayerful as
possible.

At the moment of the Consecration, Lord, you
stood up and you became one with Pierre, who
was celebrating. You were two and one at the
same time.

May your will be done, Lord. Where you will,
as you will.

May 20

A difficult morning after a few days away. I have to get the house in shape, do the wash, clean, answer the phone. It's two in the afternoon. In the silence of the empty house, I can pull myself together a bit. The doorbell! Since I can't get any rest and the time for my nap is past, I talk to the Lord.

Lord, turning to praise is difficult.

✝ *Yes, I know.*

There are tragic faces, crazy situations, Lord. That eighteen year old who just committed suicide. One can't praise you or thank you for that. It would be nothing but an empty ritual.

✝ *Not at all, Nicole. You see, on the cross I saw my torturers. Believe me, I know what people can experience at such times.*

Lord, you weren't praising God then, were you?

✝ *Yes, I was.*

But that's hard to believe. You were full of anguish. Of that I'm sure.

✝ *Yes. But you see, Nicole, I spoke to my Father. I spoke to him. Do you understand? I spoke. Even at that moment nothing was broken between him and me. That, too, is what praise is. So the torturers are there, you understand, but they are not alone.*

You want us to act as you did?

✝ *Yes. Talk to me. Talk to me.*

You help me understand, or rather you shed some light on my questions, and it's like a reve-lation. And now I'm crying, Lord. When I'm with you, I often cry, but in an odd way.

✝ *Never mind. It does not matter.*

May 21

In the truck that takes us to the Hermitage, I have a little time to think.

Lord, we haven't seen each other today.

✝ *No.*

Soon?

✝ *Yes. Do not do everything at once.*

This evening, since Pierre is away, three of us share an improvised Communion service.

Lord, you're here.

✝ *Yes. Take advantage of my presence.*

Why are you taking up residence in me? Why do you visit me? You are surely life in full measure, but why me? What do you like about me?

✝ *The élan of your heart.*

That's not much. It seems to me there are finer gifts to give you.

✢ *I do not know anything about perfect gifts. They do not interest me. What I want is to live with you, with your élan.*

You want us to love each other and for others to see that we do. Is that it, Lord?

✢ *Yes. What else would you want to do?*

May 22

I'm in the kitchen preparing a meal. It's eight o'clock in the morning. There is news on the radio about an armed robbery. The robbers were captured. I think about one of our Companions who is on the run.

Lord, what will become of them?

✝ *Why do you want to know?*

Isn't it obvious? Out of concern for them—or at least for him . . .

✝ *Do you want to be my equal?*

No . . .

✝ *Well then, do not try to know everything. For us to love each other, I need you not to know, not even to try to know.*

. . . ?

✝ *When you allow me to come into your life and work through you . . .*

In short, to use me. Say it!

✝ *No, not really. No. To be with you and in you. I draw you to myself while you draw others to me. Do you understand?*

It's a kind of contagion?

✝ *Yes.*

May 23

I wake up this morning and think about the day ahead. Lots of decisions to make without Pierre.

Lord, may your will be done. You're going to help me, but I don't know how.

✝ *Nicole, you realize that I am revealing myself to you more and more. I am not going to do your job for you, but with you. I am going to let you play your part of our duet.*

That won't be easy. There's the Companion I have to take to police headquarters at Versailles. Who knows what's going to happen there? And then there's Marc, who was drunk on my doorstep yesterday . . .

✝ *You are where you belong. You will manage. Play your part and do what you have to do.*

And you, where will you be?

✝ *I will be the light that enlightens you inwardly. Let me freely play my part, too. You know that in a duet sometimes one plays louder than the other, but we are always two. You accompany me; I accompany you.*

May 24

Lord, are you here?

✝ *Yes.*

It looks as if you're letting me handle this.

✝ *Yes.*

I feel as if I'm a boss, and a tough one at that,
but that's the way it has to be.

✝ *Go ahead.*

What are the two of us doing?

✝ *Clearing the way.*

Evening, the Eucharist with Pierre. The Lord sits down and
faces us, happy to see us, it seems.

Lord! It's good to be here and rest a while.

He appears happy to be with us.

The Host is in my hand—light, vulnerable, oh, how
vulnerable!

You're in this little bit of Host—light, fragile.
It's crazy.

✝ *Notice how light I am in your hand, Nicole. I
do not weigh anything.*

Why are you so light, Lord?

✝ *So that you can carry me better, take me with
you, keep me in a little corner of your heart. I
am handy; I do not take up any room. You, my
people, can be heavy.*

Heavy, Lord?

✝ *Carry your weight, your human heaviness;
that is how I want you to be.*

May 25

Mass at our parish church of Saint Aignan with Philippe and Benoît. On the way there I ask him:

Are you going to be there?

I'm always a little apprehensive. What if he didn't come?

After the Consecration:

✝ *Nicole, do you want me to serve as your defender, your protector?*

Yes.

✝ *I need an unconditional* yes. *I will protect you in all circumstances, but in my own way.*

Yes, Lord. Thank you.

✝ *Do not worry. I will leave you completely free, Nicole.*

And if I fail you, if sometimes I don't manage to believe, Lord?

✝ *Oh, I will wait, Nicole. I will wait for you.*

Then we're both free, Lord. In fact, we're partners.

✢ *Yes.*

Lover is a hackneyed and loaded term, but he is my lover. He knows that I hate to be under anybody's hand, to have anybody impose on me, and he gives me room to be free. I have the impression that my soul (or my being) is free to move as it will and that I go to him freely.

May 28

Three days off: the Pentecost holidays, a full house. The garden is full of sunlight, silence, too. The children will be arriving in a few minutes.

Lord, are you here?

✝ *Yes.*

It seems to me that it's been a few days since we've been together. I feel a little dull in your presence.

✝ *Nicole, I would like to ask you something. Would you like to give me a present?*

Yes.

✝ *Take time for me. Now and then you take time to call somebody up, to listen to the voice of a friend. Give me a call now and then.*

You want us to become gradually more intimate with each other?

✝ *Yes.*

I open my Bible and my eyes fall on the very beginning of the Letter to the Ephesians.

Lord, you have given me the Spirit for my inheritance. These words seem meant for me. I feel somehow predestined.

He smiles and remains silent.

I'm going to try to taste your Word a little each day.

He continues to smile in silence.

May 29

Just before dinner I went out to the far end of the garden to spend a few minutes with him. While I was making the salad, the image of a skein of wool had occurred to me several times.

> Is it from you, Lord? Is there something you want to explain to me?

> I promised to spend some time with you, so I'll continue reading.

Ephesians 1:15–23.

> Is the skein of wool really you, Lord?

> ✝ *Yes.*

> You're at one end and I'm at the other?

> ✝ *Yes. Where do you want me to be if not tied to you, to all of you? I am the one who untangles things, who pulls the thread gently, who avoids getting it all knotted up.*

May 30

Ephesians 2 and 3.

It's a beautiful day to be on the road.

> I'm enjoying life today, Lord. I feel in harmony
> with myself and with the world. Today I'm not
> letting go of you.

The images of a piece of knitting and then of a tapestry
come to me.

> We often do let go of you, Lord. The stitches
> drop and unravel back to the start of the knit-
> ting. What do you do then?

> ✝ *I try to grasp my part of the knitting firmly
> but gently so that it will still hold together.*

> But Lord, you're all-powerful. Why not have
> somebody else take up the knitting where the
> stitch dropped? Look for somebody else to do it.

> ✝ *You miss the point completely. I wait; I
> am patient; I handle my knitting gently.
> My omnipotence needs you, needs your
> weaknesses. I cannot knit or weave anything
> by myself.*

In the basilica at Saint-Benoît the Lord is seated at the foot of the altar, his hands open, surrounded by the fifteen priests who concelebrate.

June

I'm not always reasonable with you, Lord.

✝ *I do not like what is reasonable. I like things that are unreasonable.*

What do you mean?

No answer. I think I hear:

✝ *Later.*

A few minutes later I am in the middle of our secondhand store. One of the Companions, Michel, is drunk, reeling on his feet and teary-eyed. He lurches toward me: "Nicole, I have to talk to you." He weeps, he cries, he laughs, he shudders. There are a lot of people around us. Somehow we manage to make our way to the office. Michel is in a pitiful state. He weeps and clenches his fists, tells me about his wife, offers me some flowers he's carrying. I'm more and more distraught and sorry for him. He's a real case, Michel. His yelling shatters the quiet.

"Michel, do you want to pray with me?"

"Yes, I do. I just went to the chapel for the first time."

"Listen, Michel. I'm going to pray with you."

"No!" he yells. "I'll start, not you! Lord, I'm ashamed of myself! You're my only pal! Forgive me. I'm ashamed of myself! Help me, Lord!"

We conclude by saying a Hail Mary and an Our Father together. Michel cries and bows his head under the weight of his shame. I put my hand on the back of his neck, which is so weighed down, and say this silent prayer:

> Lord, look at this child. He's yours. I give him
> to you. You can help him if you will.

Humanly speaking, there was nothing I could do. Michel fell back into his raving and took off.

As I was retracing my steps on the road I had just come, the Lord said to me:

> ☩ *You have just done something unreasonable:*
> *you have put your faith in me. Yes, Nicole, I*
> *am also with Michel and in him.*

June 2

Pierre is back. The Community is nearly full except for those who prefer their liberty—the liberty, that is, to get drunk, drown their sorrows, forget. Jacky has left; Michel hasn't come back. I have a toothache and a heavy heart. The fatigue of a weekend swollen to bursting weighs on my shoulders and on my heart, too.

The image of a stream—or rather a sea of blood that inundates us—rises gently. I don't ask for anything. After the Consecration we talk to each other.

> Lord, this bath of blood . . . is it the one that washes us?
>
> ✝ *Yes.*
>
> You know, when I finish my bath I feel relaxed physically and psychologically. Is this the same?
>
> ✝ *No, it is different. I wash you of everything that is not essential. My blood washes away everything that you do not need to be concerned about.*
>
> Do you mean Michel, Jacky, all that human suffering?

✝ *Yes. I relieve you of your burdens. I make your task simpler.*

Thank you.

On my way back I feel lighter.

June 3

We've been racing around like mad, buffeted by a thousand different things to get done.

The weather is hot and stormy, but it's good to be with the Lord. Just before the Consecration the Lord enters. He stands before us clothed in white. The whiteness is radiant.

> Lord, today you're standing. You're radiant.
> Dressed in your white mantle, you dominate us.
> Why are you like that today?

> ✝ *So that you sense my presence. Just now I was in your hand and also at your side.*

Don't you have something to say?

> ✝ *When I was with my friends I was seated with them just like this, and I said nothing.*

June 4

Today he's here, but there are many people, an escort, around him.

You're not alone, Lord.

✝ *No.*

I wait. After Communion the dialogue is more intimate.

Who are those people?

✝ *Those who have helped you, supported you. Those who have led you to me. Do you believe that they are with me?*

Y . . . y . . . yes.

Lord, why are you telling us this tonight?

✝ *To make you grow, so that you realize that you are being helped and supported.*

It was like the Lord was trying to tell us that he and his friends are the world of the living.

June 5

This evening the Lord is neither standing nor sitting. We are united. It's good to pause with him.

Where are you, Lord?

✠ *In you, in Pierre. I am at home in you.*

I wait. At the moment Pierre raises the Host, the image of Christ's face from the Holy Shroud appears on the Host.

Lord, is what I'm seeing really true? I feel very calm but I can hardly believe what I'm seeing, nor do I dare say it.

✠ *Dare.*

I tell it to the others.

Why are you giving me all this, Lord?

✠ *To make all of you free of care, so that you care only for me.*

June 6

The Lord comes to sit down between Pierre and me.

Aren't you going to say something, Lord?

Later:

Don't you have anything to tell us?

✝ *It is good to be with you.*

June 7

He came to take his seat in front of the three of us. He was smiling. I asked:

Why are you smiling, Lord?

✝ *I am happy to be with you.*

But why the smile?

✝ *A smile is as good as a wealth of words.*
Smile, all of you.

June 9

You didn't come yesterday, Lord. You're here today. Where are you?

I sense that he's to my right, on the big crucifix that dominates the chapel.

What are you doing there? What are you trying to tell us?

✝ *My arms are wide open to embrace all of you, and my heart, open and bleeding, goes out to every one of you.*

Thank you. Thank you. I have found you again.

After the Letter to the Hebrews 9:15, I feel just a little upset.

✝ *Those who are called may receive the promised eternal inheritance.*

I feel called, Lord. It seems to me I've already received my share of eternity. What do you want me to do with this gift?

✝ *Nothing. Do not do anything. Let me live in you.*

June 10

On my way to the dentist this morning, I talked to him as I walked along, maybe to put the ordeal out of my mind.

> Do you want some space to live in us, live
> in me?
>
> ✝ *Yes.*

I feel in my entire being that this is what his will is all about. This evening at Mass I sense his presence. It penetrates me so fully that I feel it like a weight on the back of my neck. I become quite limp, but it's a blessed tiredness. I seem to be almost in a state of weightlessness but, simultaneously, fully alert to what's going on around me despite my numbness.

I have the impression that the Lord is telling us:

> ✝ *Make an empty space in yourself, so that I*
> *can come in. So that you can adore me.*

I'm a spoiled child.

I wait for the moment after the Consecration—a blessed time for me—to ask him:

> Why are you standing dressed all in white,
> Lord?

✝ *My cloak protects you. I have already
enfolded all of you in it. You are protected.
You are already mine.*

Stupidly, I ask:

What do I have to do, Lord?

✝ *Nothing, Nicole. Let me care for you, enfold
you, all of you.*

June 12

An outing. It feels so good to stroll without having to worry about time. Lunch with Chantal at a bistro. The tables are squeezed together, and people are exchanging glances.

> I enjoy life, Lord. But I'm still afraid that if I approach you, if I pray to you, you will take away the things that give me joy and pleasure, like getting together with my friends . . .

> ✝ *No, you are mistaken. I prolong these human moments. I am in them because I am the one who gives them to you to enjoy.*

> Then you really are the fullness of life.

> ✝ *Yes. You know that.*

June 13

Before the Consecration.

Where are you? I don't see you.

Silence.

You aren't standing, nor are you sitting beside us.

✝ *No. I am where you need me.*

Where?

✝ *Resting on your wounds. Let me stay there.*
Do not move. Let me be there, in silence.

It's as if he didn't want us to ask him any questions. As if, undisturbed, he could rest on our wounds and heal them.

June 14

There's a tension in the air today. I feel it in myself and in the Community, too.

The Lord comes to sit down at our feet.

> You, so great, why at our feet?

> ✝ *To be at the level of your hearts with my hands open. To be within your reach. Let me enter. Do not do anything. It is so simple. I am here.*

June 15

There are three of us at Mass today. During the day we had already spoken to each other.

> ✝ *There are some rough spots along the way. Do not pay any attention to them.*

That's not easy, Lord.

> ✝ *There is nothing to worry about.*

And this evening the Lord once again wraps us in his mantle.

This mantle?

> ✝ *To protect all of you. You are bruised and bleeding this evening. You need my tenderness. Let my presence come into you. Taste it right now, at this very moment.*

But why, Lord? I insist. Tell me.

> ✝ *So that you may let yourself be overcome by my love.*

Lord, my Lord.

I'm just babbling, but I have the impression of melting before him.

I know why you're telling us this tonight. Deep
down what I wanted was for you to come and
calm and console and heal all the anguish I
sensed in the others, in my brothers. But you tell
us that we've got it all wrong, that first we must
accept you, must let you come into our hearts,
and not worry about doing anything on our own.
And then you will come and act in us.

✝ *My ways are not your ways.*

June 15–16

An upset, stormy weekend. My little family lives out its minidramas, and it seems to me I have mistreated you, Lord. In the midst of these little family squalls that wear me down, I seem to have left you behind, and yet . . . you're here, I'm sure of it.

This morning at the oh-so-traditional Sunday Mass at Saint Aignan, you were there in front of us, reenacting the meal with your disciples. Once again you spoke to me. Your word reassured me. Since I didn't write anything down immediately I don't recall exactly what you said. Not wanting to misrepresent either you or myself, I won't write anything on your behalf today.

There are four of us around the table. The Lord is here. I feel his presence.

> Where are you?

> ✠ *On my knees, at the feet of each one of you.*

> What do you want to tell us?

> ✠ *I want you to look at me. I am looking at you.*

> Why are you looking at us?

> ✠ *So that you will look at me. So that we can look at one another.*

A little later, after Pierre has spoken in tongues:

> ✠ *Looking at my back is not the way to follow me. Follow me by looking me in the face, eye to eye.*

It's as if he wanted to insist that we feel his presence and to tell us that he's alive, that love shines in his eyes, that he wants to live in mutual sharing with us.

June

I just had a phone call telling me that Paul, one of the Companions for whom we were able to find a job, has hanged himself. He had gone back to drinking. What a blow! I'm physically sick at heart, and while I'm washing my hair, I break into tears.

We'll never succeed in rescuing them, Lord.

✝ *Look at me.*

. . .

✝ *Look at me. What do you read in my eyes?*

Tenderness, as if you were saying, "I know."

✝ *Yes, Nicole, I do know. But it is you I want.*

. . . !

✝ *Turn away from Paul. Look at me.*

It sounds as if you're trying to distract me, Lord.

Everything I have just written sounds crazy, and yet it's true. A little later on, in the afternoon, I'm walking to the Community and thinking how rich I am in the basic things of life: sunlight, good health, a positive outlook. It feels good to be alive at this moment.

What is poverty, Lord? I'm rich, and yet, at this moment, I believe I love you.

✠ *To be poor, Nicole, is to be rich in me.*
You and I among the rich, you and I among
the poor, you and I everywhere you go,
everywhere.

This evening at the Eucharist, there are two of us and the Lord. I feel a harmony and an especially strong sense of communion this evening.

The Lord speaks to me:

✠ *I am in you. I live in you.*

And then my untiring question:

What am I supposed to do, what are we supposed to do with you in us?

✠ *Let me speak in you.*

And later, after Pierre speaks in tongues:

✠ *I'll show you the force, the violence of*
my love.

June 19

Between sweeping up and doing dishes, before Thierry's baccalaureate exam in French and after serving lunch twice this afternoon:

✝ *You know, Nicole, I am a little like Philippe.*

. . . ! Like Philippe?

✝ *Yes. He respects your freedom. He allows you to go out to others.*

And you, you're like him?

✝ *Yes.*

Is that what your freedom is all about?

✝ *Yes.*

Lord, you're absolutely baffling. You didn't say my husband was like you. You said you were like him. It's a little backward.

June 21

On my way to the home of some friends. It's good to feel alive and on the go. Leaving the outskirts of the town behind I emerge on the open plain. The shimmering stretches of green wheat fill me with joy. The streets I've just left behind are so ugly. On the side of the road there are poppies mixed in with what I think is wheat. I have the kind of heart that always melts at the sight of these little flowers.

✝ *Look at those poppies, Nicole.*

They're beautiful, Lord. Such a strong red, and yet so fragile.

✝ *The flowers are me, you know.*

. . . ! And the rest? All the green?

✝ *The human race.*

What are you trying to tell me?

✝ *I am like those poppies. Everybody sees me. I think they also love me. But it is so easy to pull me up and toss me out of the field.*

You want me to let you stay in the fields?

June 22

On the way I walk by some gorgeous flowers. Then suddenly I have to duck to avoid a branch.

✝ *That is a sign of my kingdom.*

What do you mean?

✝ *At one moment you are admiring the flowers, and the next moment you are ducking to avoid a branch. Do this for my kingdom, too. Be supple and docile. Look up admiringly, but also bend down.*

Later on, after Communion, he makes himself clearer.

✝ *Like Mary, be flexible and gentle when you speak to me and about me.*

June 23

A day with some friends. The son of one couple and the daughter of another are living in concubinage. What an ugly word! We have lunch together. The meal is enjoyable but my heart aches. The parents seem to be happy but are still troubled by the situation. She's seventeen, he scarcely nineteen, and they're already sharing the same bed.

Lord, my heart aches.

For better or worse, Philippe and I hesitantly try to tell our own children, "It's a little early. Don't go too fast." We do it as prudently and as gently as we can.

A stroll takes us to a nearby monastery. The chapel of the Dominicans is beautiful and spare. A large figure of Christ on the cross welcomes us and towers over us.

Lord, my heart is troubled.

✝ *Yes, I know.*

Where are you?

✝ *On the cross, Nicole. I am not done carrying the cross. You know that it is for them that I am here. I am not done yet.*

Lord, tell me, what should I be doing?

✝ *Nothing. Show me to others. Speak about me.
Keep your eyes on me. Do what you have just
done with them, with me . . .*

June 24

The Eucharist. There are two of us with the Lord. I'm always a little afraid that he won't come to speak to me.

Are you going to come?

. . .

Where are you?

✝ *Where I was yesterday, on the cross.*

That must be hard.

✝ *Yes, terribly hard, but I hold on.*

How do you hold on? You look like you're bending forward so much that it can't be by the nails.

His answer comes at the moment of the Consecration.

✝ *I hold on, thanks to you and for you.*

I'm flooded with inner tears and also a few real ones.

Lord, you turn things around. You need us, our adoration, here, at this moment. Your need is exact and urgent.

June 25

The Lord is wrapped in the arms of his mother.

> What do you want to tell us?

> ✝ *When Mary carried me in her arms and when she gave me to other women, when she let others hold me, she was careful about the people she was giving me to. She was not careless. She did not put me in the arms of just anyone.*

> Do you want us to treat you just as carefully?

> ✝ *Yes.*

Later on, during the Consecration, the Lord is here—tall, living, all-powerful.

> Lord, I sense that you are standing here—great, towering over me in a way. It's so different from the way you were just a few minutes ago—tiny and precious.

> ✝ *This is me, too. I am both. Tell the others that I am both.*

June 26

From the beginning of the Mass, Jesus comes to sit beside us on my right. A small voice tells me that maybe it's only an illusion, some sort of autosuggestion. I'm torn in two: Should I listen to that small voice and pull back, or should I allow myself to savor this presence? I feel a touch of panic.

> Lord, I don't want to delude myself or you.
> Please reassure me that it's really you.

> ✢ *Do not be afraid of anything. Do not be afraid.*

> Why are you here?

> ✢ *To encourage all of you. To let you know that I am very close to you. I am a reaper like you. I am here to reap the harvest with you.*

When we leave Mass we learn that another one of the Companions has hanged himself. I'm shocked, and yet inwardly calm. While Pierre takes care of the body of the man who gave in to despair, I go to break the news to the Companions. They're all sitting there, staring at me. These men rarely show any emotion, but when I tell them what has happened, they can't handle the terrible news and break down. I had asked the Lord to put his own words in my mouth. I don't know what the men heard, but I know that peace reigns in me and that it's the Lord who gives it to me.

June 28

I continue to be at peace. This isn't the first time that I've been acquainted with people who have taken their lives. But now I'm not stricken with grief, even though I share the sorrow.

We went to the Hermitage with Pierre to bless our new home. We pray. Patrick, the Companion who discovered the body, listens to us attentively.

> ✝ *I am entering this house. Follow me. Walk behind me. Do not be afraid of anything.*

The house, our future home, is blessed. I stop for a moment in the room that will be our new chapel.

> Lord, people are saying that we're off to a bad start. I don't feel that way.

> ✝ *No, your are not starting out badly, but you are starting out poor. You share the poverty of the human condition.*

This evening at the Eucharist:

> Lord, you want us to be docile and obedient.
> You want us to be like a pawn in your hand.

✝ *No, not like a pawn. You do not understand.*

. . . ?

✝ *You follow me—all of you follow me—and you obey me, but I will not abuse you. I am treating you gently. Do not be afraid.*

Yes, Lord. I certainly felt that you were close to us. You were protecting us.

At Communion there he is in my hand, so fragile.

✝ *You see, Nicole, you do not abuse me either. You carry me gently in your hand. I do the same for you. Do not be afraid. I am here. All of you, do not be afraid.*

July 2

Robert, the Companion who committed suicide at the Hermitage, had a wife and seven children. He had spent some time in a psychiatric hospital. Humanly speaking, he was at an impasse, buried under a mountain of problems.

Robert is fine where he is. As for me, I'm at peace, even though up to now I have always reacted to the trials of the Companions very emotionally. It's not that I'm not involved, but I am at peace.

The burial today was simple and straightforward. The Companions were there, subdued and in their Sunday best. The family, dazed by its tragedy, is closed in on itself and oblivious of anybody else. The coffin begins to be lowered. I feel like giving his wife a hug as a sign of God's love for her. I walk over to her. It seems to me that for a moment her eyes brighten up. "Thank you," she murmurs. A current passed between us, but what I really wanted was that you should pass between us, Lord.

July 6

Before going to another funeral the next morning—this time with officials, firemen, flowers, and finery—I speak to him.

> We hold on by a thread. Life holds on only by a thread. A very fragile and tenuous thread is all we have to hold on to the Companions. It breaks or threatens to break all the time.

> ☩ *Yes. It is fragile and weak. The thread is very thin, Nicole. Accept it as such. I am the one who lends it strength and only I can make it resistant.*

It's true that the bond that unites me to the Lord seems terribly fine, almost invisible, and yet I feel more closely bound to him today than if I were chained to him.

A walk along some fields.

> ☩ *Look at my kingdom.*

It's a field of durum wheat, I think. The heads are gold and green, a hard green.

> Your kingdom? What do you mean?

> ☩ *Look.*

What do you mean?

✝ *The field is my kingdom. The gold is my gentleness. The green is my strength.*

Your gentleness, your strength?

✝ *Yes, the gentleness and the strength I put in you. You are the heads of grain. The field is my kingdom.*

Your word, or rather your image, fills me with joy, but also leaves me perplexed.

July 7

Today Jesus explained it to me.

Vacation at Saint-Veran. All of us happy to have a carefree week without schedules. With my feet in the stream and my eyes on the mountain, I thank the Lord for so much goodness, for everything.

Your kingdom is really beautiful, Lord. Thank you.

✝ *Yes, my kingdom is beautiful.*

Not all of it. Here and now, at this moment, yes.

✝ *No, all of it. Look at the stream.*

I look at it. The water runs down over rocks and stones. Here and there are pieces of dead wood.

The water—the stream—is you?

✝ *Yes.*

The wood, the rocks, the stones are us?

✝ *Yes.*

There are some that aren't even moistened by you.

✛ *True. But, nonetheless, you can see that it is all beautiful.*

Yes, Lord.

✛ *This is my kingdom.*

As I'm coming down the mountain, I reflect on this image when I'm not thinking about how much my feet hurt or worrying about falling. The Lord tells us not to stop at any one rock or stone. Each one is part of the whole. It came as a response to the question that I ask him so often when I read in the papers about all the catastrophes with their suffering and death.

It's an answer, Lord, but not an explanation.

✛ *I do not explain.*

What do you do then?

✛ *I speak. I suggest.*

July 8

From the paths the mountain is lovely. Philippe and our friend Christiane are happy. So am I.

We resume our conversation.

> I'd like to have you explain things to me. As long as you're talking to me, why don't you explain things to me?

> ✝ *I cannot. It is my kingdom, our kingdom. If you understood it, it would become your domain.*

What it comes down to is that the Lord needs our trust, our childlike trust. If he is to be able to work, to act, to live with us, he needs us not to know.

July 9

Mass at nine in the sacristy. There are only six of us—three tourists and three elderly women from the neighborhood. The priest celebrates Mass as if he were in a cathedral jammed with people. His voice rings out loud and strong for his meager congregation. It's a little out of scale, and yet, the Mass is moving. The Lord, attentive as always, comes and wraps me in his presence. He understands, and I feel safe in his arms. The experience is tender and simple. I can only respond to him with tears that have no sadness in them.

Why me? Why all this?

✝ *Because I have chosen you.*

Up to now I have always been exasperated by a certain way of speaking. The way nuns talked about Jesus—as if he were their lover—rubbed me the wrong way. It seemed to me that they were putting on airs. I always thought of the Song of Songs as reserved for a certain elite, but now I suspect that a complete relationship (I almost said a sexual relationship) with the Lord is possible. It's not only possible for a John of the Cross, but it's offered to the mother of a family, which is what I am, to a perfectly ordinary Christian woman like me. It's staggering!

We move on to another spot. It's just as beautiful. There's a rock nearby. The stream flows over it, boiling up and covering it completely in transparent water.

The Lord gives me a knowing glance.

> ✝ *The rock is you, Nicole.*

The water running over it is you, Lord?

> ✝ *Yes, it is. What do you see?*

I see myself clearly under the water. I see both of us, but to me it's the water that's fascinating.

The Lord adds:

> ✝ *Show me to others. Reveal me. Let yourself be immersed in me. Show me to others.*

As I cast my gaze over the stream, I notice other rocks. They're beautiful and nicely located where they are. I realize that I'm no better than the rock beside me. I'm just wetter, more immersed. I'm different, not better.

July 10

Walking through meadows full of flowers. The mountain has changed. The harmony that reigns between us, the beauty of the landscape, makes me want to praise and thank the Lord. I feel very human and happy to be alive on this earth.

And you, Lord, where are you?

✝ *I am here.*

You know, I get the feeling that when I really throw myself into the present moment, I forget the spiritual world. I have the impression that there are two worlds—the world of humans and the one that belongs to you—even though I know that's not true. When I'm happy, as I am now, where are you?

✝ *I am here, but I get out of the way a little.*

You get out of the way?

✝ *Yes. You do the same with Laurette, Philippe, the boys. You stay in the background when they are with their friends or with others. I do the same.*

Thank you, Lord. I can understand that. I had asked you for another way to say "I love you," but you never gave me one.

✝ *No.*

You won't give me another way?

✝ *No.*

Why not?

✝ *You do not need another way to say it.*

? ! ? ! . . .

✝ *Does Philippe say it?*

No.

✝ *See, you do not need it.*

What do you mean?

✝ *If you say "I love you" to someone, the risk is that you will stop there. When you say "I love you," you need to add, "Now do what you want."*

? ! ? ! . . .

✝ *Love, you know, is a space. It is an ample space that leaves the other free. Free to develop, to go away, to draw close. The essential thing, Nicole, is to be linked with one another.*

July 11

While I'm walking in the woods, the idea of a musical score comes back to me. We treasure the silence, the time, the space we have to ourselves. I want to ask him questions, but I'm always afraid that he won't answer me.

> You want me to play my part of our duet, but you know that I'm very vulnerable. I'm sensitive to the beauty of people and things, to misfortune, to suffering. I'm vulnerable, don't you see? And what about you?
>
> ✝ *I am invincible.*
>
> And I'm . . . vulnerable.
>
> ✝ *Yes.*
>
> Is that really the way it is?
>
> ✝ *Yes.*
>
> If I let you play your part, will you make me invincible, too?
>
> ✝ *Yes, and you already know that.*

A few moments later:

> Do you offer to play your part often?

✝ *Yes.*

But people don't want you to?

✝ *No. They do not even know what I am offering them.*

That must hurt you. I feel bad when I see people being mistreated, especially if they're being physically abused. That sort of thing disgusts me. But I suppose you feel more suffering than disgust for those who mistreat others.

✝ *Yes, that is true. I feel bad, bad for them. If only they knew.*

You feel that bad?

✝ *Yes, very bad.*

Later on:

Tell me, Lord, you don't judge, do you?

✝ *I feel bad.*

I come back to the topic obstinately:

If you don't judge, if you love to that extent, is there a hell, Lord?

✝ *Why are you so concerned about my Father's affairs?*

? ! ? ! . . .

July 12

We set out at the crack of dawn. My head is swimming, my heart pounding. We climb. This kind of mountain sickness is hard to take; everything is fuzzy. I'd love to speak to the Lord, but I can't manage. I content myself with putting one foot in front of the other and hope that I can get to the summit. We make it. The mountain is rugged and barren. There are rocks everywhere. It amazes me to see some little flowers managing to survive on these arid heights. For the nth time I say to myself, "How beautiful!"

✝ *Yes, you are right. They are beautiful. Be like them.*

What do you mean?

✝ *Be what you love in them.*

! ! They're simple and bright, Lord, like eyes you'd like to dive into.

✝ *Be these little flowers among the rocks. Content yourselves with being these little specks of light.*

July 13

It's good to live and let oneself live.

The present moment is good, Lord.

✝ *Grasp it. Live it to the fullest. I am in the present moment. I am the present.*

July 14

We have to climb to get to Mass. On the ascent I feel a bit distracted. I tell him so.

> It doesn't look as if I care much about hurrying
> off to you today.

No answer.

The Mass begins. The church is full. The celebration is simple and prayerful.

> Thank you for Christiane, for Philippe. Thank
> you for this harmonious week.

At the moment of Consecration I feel myself invaded anew. I sense a weight on the back of my neck, my eyes fall shut. Twice, my eyelids have a hard time opening to see the bread and wine elevated above the altar. It is not I who adore the Lord, but I am turned into someone who adores and offers. I'm still myself, very much alive, not lacking anything.

> My Lord and my God.

> I'm beginning to discover you, Lord, even
> though I knew you before. I went to church
> regularly. But now everything is different.

✝ *Yes. You did not know me well. I was like clothing you put on inside out.*

! ! And now, Lord?

✝ *You are wearing it right-side out.*

Amen.

July 15

I take leave of Philippe and Christiane at the station. During the boring train ride I recite the Our Father and the Hail Mary.

"Pray for us sinners . . ." It always sticks a little in my throat when I say *sinners*. I don't think of myself as a sinner. Tell me, Lord, is it a lack of humility not to think of myself as a sinner?

✝ *No. Once again, you misunderstand.*

If it's not a lack of humility, Lord, what is it? A lack of what?

✝ *A lack of obedience to the freedom of my love. A lack of flexibility in allowing yourself to grow through me.*

Yes, I understand. *Sinners* isn't negative. It's an invitation to grow, to let oneself grow in you.

A silly, childish question runs through my mind.

Why *sinner,* Lord? It would be so much simpler for you if we weren't sinners.

✝ *Nicole, my Father and I have no need for puppets.*

July 16

Nothing. No, not nothing. A lot. I have the impression that I'm accompanied.

July 17

Are you here, Lord?

✝ *You know I am.*

What are you doing?

✝ *I am letting you live. Take advantage of it.*

And it's true. In my friends' house, the sort of house one dreams about, surrounded by lavender and open space, I am as happy as can be. I let myself be spoiled like a pampered only child in the fold of Annie's and Gabriel's hearts.

This is good, Lord. Thanks to them, to you.

✝ *Take it. I am giving it to you for your enjoyment.*

July 18

Up at 6:30. I study Baudelaire. Suddenly I hear bells on the nearby mountain. A flock of sheep comes down the road in the morning light. The shepherd is behind them, leaning on his staff. He lets the flock graze. The scene is biblical. I have the impression that the Lord says to me:

> ✞ *You see—all of you see—I let you go before me to live, to taste, and to eat of life in the moments I give you.*

July 19

A moment of silence far from talk and chatter.

> It's good, Lord, to walk along the path above
> this little village. Your nature is beautiful. I
> benefit from it, you know.

> ✝ *It is good that you do.*

> Are you giving me these full and blessed days to
> arm me and nourish me for tomorrow?

> ✝ *Nicole, I am not a schoolmaster.*

> What are you, then?

> ✝ *A revealer. I open your eyes and reveal things*
> *to you as you go along.*

The image of something thrown into the water and making
bigger and bigger circles takes shape in my mind.

> Could I say that your way is to work in concen-
> tric circles?

> ✝ *Yes, it is a bit like that.*

> Tell me, Lord, could it be that those waves get
> bigger and bigger until they touch other shores?

Is what you reveal to me meant for others, Lord? Will you tell me?

✝ *That will happen. Do not fret about it.*

Will you let me know?

✝ *That will happen.*

July 20

The sun beats down on me on the road to the village. I speak to him.

> The road I'm taking is a little like the one you set before me, Lord. The thing to do is to walk and we'll meet you at the end?

> ✝ *No.*

> Why not?

The image, or rather the presence, of the Lord makes itself felt. He stands in front of me, his arms open.

> You're not at the end of the road, but in front of me here. Is that what you're trying to tell me?

> ✝ *Yes.*

> Are your arms open to carry me when the going is too hard?

> ✝ *Not only then. When you are getting along well, too. Free of charge.*

The Lord seems to smile and be a little amused at me. I stop at the little church of Moustiers. In one big lump, I pour out my thanks to him, my prayers for pardon, my intentions. It's standard prayer, nothing special. I come out of the church at peace. The peace is interior.

On the road back he asks me:

✝ *Why do you want to pass me up? Why do you want to walk ahead of me?*

You're right, Lord. I'm anxious to show my little notebook to Gabriel and to some other people, and to tell them about my encounters with you.

✝ *You are going too fast.*

The refrain from an old love song comes to my lips:

"This is just for you. Don't tell anyone that love has driven me mad . . ."

Now the Lord is definitely amused.

Am I encroaching on your space, Lord? Is this your part of the duet?

✝ *Yes.*

July

An old priest celebrates Mass. The church is full but we are not together. A moralizing, threatening sermon dwells on the evils of our age—above all, sex. It grates on me. In part, what he says is true, but it leaves me tense. To calm down a bit I let prayer rise in me even while I go on listening.

At the Consecration the Lord appears above the altar, his arms open to embrace the whole crowd.

> Lord, I would have loved to see a tiny bit of your mantle behind the words of the preacher.

> ✞ *Nicole, that is his way of saying that I am feeling bad.*

You're feeling bad?

> ✞ *It is difficult. People are difficult.*

This touches my heart.

> Lord, I sense how weighed down you are. I want to help you carry your burden. What should I do?

> ✞ *Keep on being the little flowers of my kingdom.*

July 23

Back to the fold, to the Community. It's always hard for me to come back again to these sad barracks where there are so many problems every day. Going from one planet to another is always tough, and the little voice that I now know so well chants, "What are you doing here, Nicole? You're wasting your time. They'll do just fine without you." It takes some effort for me to get on board the moving train again.

At the Eucharist I don't experience the usual joy of celebrating Mass in this chapel that we love so much.

> I'm not calm and peaceful, Lord. You will have to accept me as I am. It's rather hard, you know.

> ✠ *Do not be afraid.*

At the Consecration:

> ✠ *I am leading you along. I am taking you with me. Do not be afraid.*

> But I'd love to know where you're taking me. Is it nice there? Is the place you're taking us to beautiful?

> ✠ *You do not need to know. That would not serve any purpose.*

July 23

Lord, the *Compagnons du Partage* is a veritable theater. I'm gone for two weeks, and there's a new cast and a new show.

✝ *I am lending you these men. Do not make plans.*

July 24

✝ *Be like children. Let go.*

Lord, you keep saying that all the time. It seems
to me that we are letting go. When you say
you're lending us the Companions, do you mean
Pierre, too?

✝ *Yes, I am lending them to you.*

Why don't you want us to make plans for them?

✝ *Because I know what you need. I know what
is right for them. If you make your own plans,
you keep me from giving presents to you and
to them.*

July 25

On the way to the Community I talk to him.

> Thinking over everything you say to us, Lord,
> it seems to me that you want us to be as light
> as possible.

✝ *Yes.*

> You want us to hold on to nothing, to nobody?

✝ *That is correct.*

> I have the impression that I'm like a sea that's
> always in motion. I feel a little seasick.

✝ *Why? Let the men come and go in this*
> *Community. I have already told you: be like*
> *leaves in the wind. Anchor yourself in me. I*
> *am the fixed point, the solid ground. You will*
> *not feel this heartache anymore.*

> When we get right down to it, then, you come
> first, Lord. In a certain way, the Companions
> come second.

✝ *Yes.*

> So I'm going in the wrong direction when I'm
> concerned about them first of all?

✝ *Yes.*

Eucharist at the chapel.

> ✝ *Leave me free to act in you. Let me be completely free.*

Are we hindering you or slowing you down, Lord?

> ✝ *No, not really, but you are not resting enough on me and in me.*

July 26

Mass. Three Companions are here and a woman who is a friend of the Community. The Lord is present from the start of the Mass. He moves about and goes from one to the other.

Why are you moving about this evening, Lord?

And then all at once I am gripped by doubt. What if I made this all up? What if it's autosuggestion? What if . . . what if . . . ? I know this ditty well. It leaves me in a state of distress. I try to quiet myself interiorly.

My heart grows warm. It pounds a little, and I hear the Lord say:

✝ *Tell them what I am telling you.*

But what if it's only me, Lord?

✝ *Tell them.*

I relate our dialogue, even though I find the presence of the Companions intimidating. I dive in.

Lord, you usually don't move around so much.
Why are you so active this evening?

✝ *Because I am movement.*

Do you think that we're not moving?

✝ *Do not mark time. Do not ask too many questions. Get going. Throw yourselves into it.*

Ah!

✝ *You say that I am living. Well then, since I look after you, get going.*

July 27

The Lord is present in the back of the chapel.

You're behind us, Lord.

✝ *Yes, so you can feel me. I support you. I am here.*

July 28

The Lord comes and sits next to me. On my right. As close and warm and living as Philippe on my left, or as the Companions. He's seated like us, nothing more. His presence warms me and fills me. My head becomes heavy. Once again I feel like dozing off.

When it comes time to eat the bread and drink from the cup, he seems to draw apart.

Tell me, where are you going?

✝ *I allow you to taste my body. I am
inexhaustible.*

What Pierre just said is true: "I am inexhaustible." It's not in my head. It's not my imagination. It is he. I feel myself engulfed in his presence.

✝ *Plunge into me. Immerse yourself in my presence. Happy or unhappy, you are all bathed
in my love. I am inexhaustible.*

July 29

7:30 in the morning. A telephone call from Pierre. There's been a ruckus among the Companions. Five of them have broken the rules of the Community. What are we going to do? It's 8:30. We go to the chapel to ask he who leads us.

Prayer. Question.

What should we do?

Answer: Letter to the Colossians 4:2–6.

> ✝ *"Devote yourselves to prayer, keeping alert in it with thanksgiving. . . . Conduct yourselves wisely toward outsiders, making the most of the time. Let your speech always be gracious, seasoned with salt, so that you may know how you ought to answer everyone."*

Thank you, Lord. I wanted to bawl them out, but we didn't do anything of the kind. All five have left, destination unknown. Some said good-bye, others nothing. Not a sign, not a word of thanks. "You mess up, you pay for it." That's all there is to it. There's nothing more to say. You get what you deserve.

I recall what the Lord said to us:

✝ *You patch, you mend.*

But the garment belongs to you, Lord.

At the Eucharist this evening his message extends the gospel of the day.

✝ *Be simple and little.*

Tell us more, Lord.

✝ *Live. Take things—deeds, people—simply.*

Why do you insist on this simplicity, Lord?

✝ *Because that makes the task easier for you. Do not complicate things. Be simple. I will give the increase in due time. If you are small and simple I will be able to act big and tall behind you, after you.*

July 30

Not very receptive tonight. I think more about my black skirt, which I like very much, than I do about placing myself before him in silence.

> Lord, here in front of you I feel a little frivolous.
> I'm having some trouble entering deeply into
> myself in order to come to meet you.

At the Consecration it's always the same thing. He's here, living, present, attentive.

> ✝ *Plunge into me. I am invincible. I have over-*
> *come everything at every moment, everything*
> *that is—the beautiful, the good, the ugly, the*
> *malicious, the violent. I am here, living.*

July 31

It's a lovely day. We have the plans for our new house. Pierre leaves to lie down. The Companions are at the farm, glad to be working. The Beauce is still golden and ripe in the sun. Everything in me is singing for the joy of being alive, for seeing the others serene and, if not happy, at least relaxed and more or less at peace.

I'm getting the house ready to welcome my Laurette, whom I haven't seen for a month, and my friend Martine and her children. My heart is singing for joy, and then, as I'm out doing my shopping, I suddenly encounter the nasty, spiteful face of Jean-Luc. He has just turned on a friend and must feel belligerent—and guilty, too. It's the stroke of a knife in the midst of our harmony.

✝ *Nicole, love him.*

Look here, Lord, it's not all that easy. He turned on me, too, remember?

✝ *Yes, I know. Do not be afraid. Pray for him. Love him.*

Do you realize what you're asking of me?

✝ *Yes.*

How do you want me to act?

✝ *I will go with you. Do not be afraid. I will help you. You will see. Do not do anything except pray for him.*

August 1

✞ *I have overcome everything.*

Everything, Lord? Look at the papers. Listen to the radio. Everything that's going on, the crimes, the wars . . .

✞ *Everything. It is not enough to believe it. You have to live out that belief, too.*

How, Lord? Are you going to give me a tape recorder so I can play it when the going gets tough?

✞ *No, you have to live it. Do not wait to confirm it. Live it ahead of time, not afterward.*

Why? You know how hard it is to live it.

✞ *Ahead of time, so that I can intervene. So that you can let me go with you. To act and speak and live with you.*

Mass at the retreat house at Thieulin a little while later. At the Consecration it's as if Christ were here once again, years later. He's always the same. Time shrinks to the point at which yesterday and today are one. I have the impression of seeing the Lord and being with him on Holy Thursday. The Last Supper isn't reproduced. It lives anew. It is.

August 4

✝ *I will heap joys on you.*

I believe you, Lord. But tell me, how are you going to accomplish it? You know very well that life, that the world, is sometimes difficult. Explain it to me.

✝ *When you talk about your studies in Paris, about what you discovered, sometimes at the cost of great effort, you claim that you have accumulated a wealth that belongs to no one but you, that no one can steal from you. Am I right?*

Yes, Lord, you're right.

✝ *Well, I am your treasure. I am in you. You know that. No one can take me from you.*

But to heap joys upon me? How are you going to do that?

✝ *You are going to accomplish that, not I. On any occasion, at every moment, you can come looking for me and find me.*

What will you do?

✝ *When you are happy, I will be happy with you. When you cry, I will cry with you.*

And when it's very heavy-going?

✝ *I will carry you. I will give you someone to help you.*

You have chosen me, Lord. You seem to want to cover me in your light, to clothe me in your mantle, in yourself.

✝ *Yes, that is right.*

To do what, Lord?

✝ *To shine out and to proclaim me.*

You could have chosen a more gifted servant than me. I'm not particularly gentle or peaceful.

✝ *I will teach you.*

What it comes down to is that I only have to follow you and let go of myself.

✝ *Yes.*

August 5

We are—I am—a little dichotomous. Two
worlds: that of the human, that of the spiritual.

✝ *No, you are mistaken.*

What do you mean?

✝ *I give you these two worlds to live in, and you
must shuttle continuously between the two,
binding them together. Certainly you can see
that if you do not do this, you can die. You
have to keep going from one to the other.*

Later:

✝ *Now you can see that your idea about eternity
was wrong.*

! . . . ! . . .

✝ *You tell me that the thought of my eternity
makes you feel faint.*

Yes, that's true.

✝ *Why? My eternity is the day when you will no
longer have to shuttle. The two worlds will be
only one.*

August 6

Monique, Nicole, two Companions.

> ✝ *I walk with you. I am at your side. I help you.*

Lord, you have so much to carry. You want us to give you our burdens, but your cross is already very heavy.

> ✝ *It is even heavier when you do not give me your burdens.*

August 7

The Lord is here, on his knees before each one of us. His face before me—without any distinguishing features, but powerful and compelling—seems to pull me toward him. I'm inwardly at peace. I have the impression that I'm sinking or melting into him.

> The world is in such bad shape. The troubles and the sorrows of the Companions . . . What a hard time we have understanding.

> ✝ *Pray for what you do not understand. I have not given you the world so you can dominate it by your intelligence. I have given you a field to cultivate. The world that is so close to you—the Companions, Pierre, Philippe, your children, your little world . . . For the rest, you do not understand, so pray.*

August 8

The Gospel of Matthew 9:18–26.

> This woman and her faith, Lord . . . Isn't her
> faith a kind of magic? Is it as true today as yes-
> terday that all we need is faith?
>
> ✝ *Yes.*
>
> For me, too?
>
> ✝ *Yes. Are you not sure about that? When have I
> not answered your prayers?*

I think about it, and it's true: the Lord has always answered
my prayers.

> Yes, Lord, it's true. I have a hard time saying it,
> but it's true. You answer our prayers when we
> ask with all our heart and when it's urgent.
>
> ✝ *Yes, Nicole. Yes.*
>
> Lord, I'm not asking you for anything for Pierre
> today. I'm not asking you to cure him. I didn't
> do it for Monique, remember?
>
> ✝ *Yes, I know.*

What about Pierre, Lord?

✝ *Do not fret. Do not fret about anything. You have not asked for anything for him. That is all right. Wait. Do not fret about anything.*

August 9

✝ *Be like children. Stay that way.*

Lord, why do you insist on this?

✝ *Because if you left me free, as children do, I would be able to show you marvelous things and give you gifts.*

Heaviness and sadness today. I'm not too sure where it comes from. I feel like showing my little notebook to a friend. Pierre tells me not to. I'm going to try to obey, but I don't feel like it. I have the impression that the two of us, the Lord and I, are having an argument. We're not getting along very well. I try to say prayers of praise. It grates.

During the day this mood slackens, and this evening at Mass, the Lord is seated beside us, his elbows on his knees, terribly present.

✝ *Speak to them, Nicole.*

I say that he's here, sitting with us to comfort us and to tell us that he's with us, that he's here not to look at us, but to act with us, in us. It's powerful.

Lord, you're looking at me. What do you want?

✝ *Do you want to follow me?*

Look for yourself, Lord. Am I doing anything else?

✝ *You feel like resisting. Let go of yourself.*

The image of a channel appears with water pouring out of it.

Are you the channel?

✝ *Yes.*

And am I the water?

✝ *Yes.*

Why?

✝ *Let go of yourself. Let me channel the water.*
I am the one who directs the way the water
flows. Be willing to let go of yourself. You
will see.

How can I resist him when I sense such care and such respect at the same time? I haven't the least inclination to obey him, but I'm going to do it, for I can't refuse him. That wouldn't be right, and yet . . .

August 11

A minivacation with Philippe and Laurette. On the beach.
When we arrived the sky was gray and it was raining.
Suddenly it's all swept away and the sea changes color
constantly.

> ✝ *Be adaptable, like the surface you're looking
> at.*

. . . !

> ✝ *It changes, it moves, it turns red, it
> sparkles . . .*

Yes, I see. So you want me to let go and be
completely at your mercy?

> ✝ *Yes.*

That's all!

August 13

A reading from the beginning of the First Letter of John. I balk at 1:10: "If we say that we have not sinned, we make him a liar, and his word is not in us."

The next day the phrase becomes clear: "Those who have been born of God do not sin" (1 John 3:9).

But, Lord, I'm still a bit confused.

✝ *In what you have just read you have the front and the back of the fabric.*

The fabric is you. It's in your hands. And sometimes we see one side, and sometimes the other. Is that it?

✝ *Yes.*

August 14

First Letter of John 3:22:

"And we receive from him whatever we ask, because we obey his commandments and do what pleases him."

This is difficult to understand and accept. I don't understand it very well.

✝ *That is right; you do not.*

It's the *whatever* that bothers me. You don't grant everything, do you?

✝ *I do not grant just anything.*

Who is going to tell us how to ask for what pleases you?

✝ *The Holy Spirit. You know that.*

But wait a minute. If we are to ask for what pleases you, aren't we just playing a game of hide-and-seek?

✝ *Not at all. Do not get upset. I will help you understand.*

August 15

The church is full. Three priests are concelebrating, and the overall effect is painful. It's more of a show than a celebration. I find it hard to take. I imagine momentarily how the space between the altar and the people could be filled with singing and dancing.

After Communion I receive the answer to yesterday's question.

> ✟ *Requests are made in the setting of a relationship between you and me, between me and all of you.*

> ! ! . . . What does that mean?

> ✟ *You do not ask Philippe or the children for any old thing at any old time. It is the same way with me. You did not understand yesterday because you forgot what is essential: the relationship.*

That's true. Now I understand better. Thank you.

August 19

Jesus is in the chapel with Mary.

Why are both of you here?

✝ *So that you may pay attention to Mary.*

What do you mean?

✝ *Do what she did. She always said yes.*

August 20

Jesus and Mary. They hold hands, and the way they do it reveals the great love that unites them.

You're both here again? What is it you want me to grasp?

✝ *Be like her. Effective like her.*

Effective?

✝ *Yes. Present, gentle, self-effacing, but still radiant. Be like her.*

August 22 and 23

A difficult day. At the Hermitage the Companions haggle, criticize, attack.

I listen to them and am a bit astounded and shaken. I try to hand it all over to the Lord, but it's difficult.

I meet with them again the next day, and this time I do the talking and try to clarify things. Everything becomes calm as if by magic. Pierre, who is about ten miles away, is helping us with his prayers. In addition to yesterday's bad humor being gone, I was able to put some home truths across to them very firmly. We parted as friends and in a good mood.

> Thank you, Lord. You helped me when I was all alone.

> ✝ *I hold you in my hand.*

> Thank you.

> ✝ *The Companions lead you to me, Nicole. What matters is not being loved by them, but loving me. They are the ones who lead you to me in this moment of our heart-to-heart exchange. Let yourself be led by them along my paths.*

August 25

A large gathering of all the staff and the Companions. Some of them have a very difficult time sharing the same living quarters.

Mass. Jesus is here. He's big, almost too big for this tiny chapel. He's standing and takes us all in with his gaze.

✝ *I am here. I arrived here ahead of you. Do not be afraid. I am here, and I am first. Let me always be in the first place.*

After a fairly peaceful meal, one of the difficult Companions decides to leave. Our problems are taken care of, at least for the time being.

August 26

The Lord is here. At the moment of the Our Father, he opens his arms wide.

Why are you doing that, Lord?

✝ *Because we have the same Father. Make your requests of my Father. I am with you.*

August 27

I have a hard time being receptive to him. Our two boys have just gotten back from a two-month stay in the States.

After Communion I have the nerve to ask the Lord:

Are we good guardians?

✝ *Yes.*

He smiles.

Is something lacking?

✝ *Yes. Really have the heart of a child. Ask the way children do. I will do wonderful things. Believe that I can.*

August 28

✝ *Do not be afraid. It is not only my hands I stretch out toward you, but my arms as well. I walk with you. I meet you faithfully. Do not be afraid.*

August 29

The whole family is here. Three Companions. The consecrated Host is on the table. All of us are standing around it.

✝ *I am malleable, infinitely malleable.*

I'm a little afraid to say this to the others.

✝ *Tell them.*

I say: "I am malleable like the clay that is to be molded. I will fill what is empty, straighten out all that is rough and crooked in you. Let me simply draw close to your hearts. I am moldable."

September

The Lord is walking along a road. He bends over to take something in his arms.

What are you carrying?

✝ *All of you. You need to be carried. You are the ones I especially care for. I hold you close to my heart.*

After Communion the Lord tells us:

✝ *I know what I am doing.*

September

From the beginning of the Mass it's as if I'm wrapped in a cloak. Even though it's thick, heavy, and full, it's light. It's as if I'm a part of him. He lacks nothing, and yet no one is excluded. Those I carry in my heart, the men and women for whom we pray, are with me. I have the deepest desire to let myself sink into this numbness. I try not to fall off my bench, but the back of my neck feels heavier and heavier. It's a gift from the Lord—at least I think it is.

> You're beyond words. I can't describe you, but I feel you, and I know you're present. Thank you. Do you have something special to say to us?

> ✝ *Yes. I clothe you with my garment. I make you invulnerable. Do not be afraid. I have already told you that. I have chosen you; I protect you; I am leading you. Do not be afraid. I am doing it.*

There's something infinitely sweet and yet very strong in this presence that envelops me.

September 4

His presence is so strong that I feel like dozing off right at the beginning of Mass. I resist.

A deep and all-embracing peace spreads through me. I bless the Lord and thank him. After Communion, he invades me, invades all of us.

> ✝ *I embrace you. Just as you are, with your limi-*
> *tations and weaknesses. I do not want you to*
> *be anything else. I want you with me.*

September 6

A force seems to descend on the Host at the moment of the Consecration. It's hard to put into words. It's like a great weight, but still light and airy. Gradually it becomes one with the Host. It's comforting.

What are you trying to tell us, Lord?

✝ *Feel this force and believe. You know and believe that I am present at this moment. Believe in me, all of you. Believe in me, the Living One.*

It's so strong that it's beyond words.

September

A friend confides in me. The load she has to carry and endure is so heavy that my heart aches as I listen to her. We are at the limits of what is human, on the brink of madness. I listen and feel faint for her.

✠ *Nicole, believe that I am here.*

So I simply and silently made this act of faith. Silently . . . Happy are those who can share their faith, their hope.

> I was embarrassed to do so, Lord, so I said nothing about the riches I receive from you. All I did was what you told me to do: believe.

> In the darkness, bereft of any human solution, I believe. You know how to dwell in the silence, Lord, so if that is what you will, play your part. All I can do is keep silent and call on you.

September 13

I entrust the Companions to him.

> ✝ *Forget them.*

Why, Lord?

> ✝ *You have come to see me, to spend time with
> me. Forget them.*

I have a hard time concentrating on him. That will come.
I'm just beginning.

A little later:

> ✝ *Do you want to be my servant?*

Yes.

> ✝ *I will make you a queen, the queen of my
> kingdom.*

An invisible kingdom?

> ✝ *Invisible and visible.*

The peace that dwells in me is profound. I experience it all
evening. If a doctor friend of mine were to read what I have

written, he would probably send me off to the psychiatric ward, but he would be mistaken. This peace really comes from the Lord.

September 16

Manuel, a Companion, is with me. In silence. It's a gift.

I entrust the Companions to the Lord, those who are present and those who are absent. Also Catherine and her difficulties at work.

> ✝ *Do not worry. She will soon be free of them.*

And then I look at the Host in its golden monstrance.

> ✝ *Do not worry. I will help you understand. I will look through your eyes.*

Tell me what you mean, Lord.

> ✝ *The Host you see is encircled with gold. The gold is my gaze on humanity. I will come to look at people along with you, to help you see them as I do. I do not belittle your intuition, your way of looking at things. It is just as true as the Host you are looking at. I will come and wrap it in mine.*

Amen.

September 17

There's a great calm or, rather, a repose. I'm drained and empty this evening, and in the chapel, kneeling next to Manuel, I offer the Lord all those I carry.

The Lord comes to us with a smile and puts his arms around us. I fall into a kind of weightlessness. I feel neither my body nor my joined hands. I stammer. That's all I can do today. As I leave the chapel, peace. "Do not be afraid." The other day a priest friend of mine, Father Guédou, called to tell me about his close brush with death: "We make everything so complicated. The Evil One puts on a lot of nice faces, but everything is so simple. When you're close to death, there's very little that matters."

September 18

Lord, here in your presence I feel scattered, a little diluted by all the people and things I'm involved with.

✝ *A little, yes. I am only lending you these people, these faces, these events. What I give you—have already given you—is myself.*

September 19

One of the Companions, perhaps the best one, got plastered. I'm heartbroken and am starting to feel faint again. The Lord is here. He draws close to my face and smiles at me. Yesterday's words come back: "I am lending them to you."

September 20

✝ *I will make your house grow. Do not be afraid. I will do it.*

Do you mean the Community, Lord?

✝ *Yes. I will make it grow.*

September 21

Lord, we're told we're not supposed to judge.
But we can't avoid judging. "Don't condemn" I
can understand. But "Don't judge" doesn't make
any sense to me at all.

✝ *I have given you your capacity to judge. Use
it. Completely. Do not hesitate, but do not
pigeonhole people by your judgment.*

Please explain that more fully.

✝ *Because I am in them, too, in my own way,
even if you do not see it or even sense it at
times. Do not limit what I can do, say, or
accomplish in them. Do you understand?*

September 22

A heavy and difficult day. Too many things to do. I feel so exhausted that I begin to cry. The Lord smiles. He walks down the steps and comes to meet me.

> ✝ *Do you want to continue to be my little servant? I will make you a queen.*

Yes, I do.

September 28

During my time of Adoration he came and, with a smile, very gently took me in his arms. It was simple and comforting.

✝ *Carry on. Do not be afraid. I will spoil you.*

Before we part, I ask him:

Send out harvesters, Lord. There are not enough of us. We asked you for a driver and you gave us one. A solution for one of the Companion's problems, and you gave us that, too. Now I'm asking for harvesters. You realize that with Pierre gone for a few days I can hardly keep my head above water.

✝ *I will take care of it, Nicole. Do not be afraid. I will give you what you need.*

October 1

This time I'm all by myself in this privileged place. He begins.

> ✝ *You see. You have nothing to be afraid of. You used to be afraid that this half-hour of Adoration would be too long. Now you know how quickly the time passes with me.*

I'm sorry, Lord. You're right. I find peace when I'm with you, and when you talk to me, you put me back together again. You give me an invisible solidity.

The Lord's smile is full of tenderness, with perhaps just a little touch of weariness.

> Is my head or my heart too impenetrable, Lord?

> ✝ *No, not really. But you are a bit negligent.*

> ! ! What do you mean?

> ✝ *You get colds—and now you have just come down with the flu—because you forget to put on a coat. You move from one place to another without giving any thought to what you are wearing.*

You mean I'm forgetting to clothe myself with you?

✝ *Yes. I am like a coat. Take the time to clothe yourself with it, to slip it on.*

Why?

✝ *So that I may protect you, and also act in you and around you.*

October 2

After a half-hour with Jesus in the chapel, I go back into the night, dead tired. The day was terribly full. At home, the doorbell rings. It's Jean-Luc, an ex-Companion, drunk, sneering. He yells at me. There is hatred in his voice, something diabolic about the way he looks at me. I try to keep calm, but my heart goes cold. When Philippe gets home he calmly gets him settled down. Jean-Luc lowers his head, excuses himself, and takes off.

The children were present. We talk about it at table. Laurette says:

"I know why he insulted Mommy. I get like that, too. When I'm ashamed of myself, I yell at her."

And Laurette's only eleven years old! We talk about the poor, God, religion.

Thierry, who's sixteen:

"What you're doing for the Companions is good, but it's useless."

"Useless?"

"Yes, useless. And that's why you should keep on doing it."

Benoît adds:

"It's not Jean-Luc you're saving; you're saving yourself."

There's no chill in my heart any longer. Quite the contrary. My children restored me to peace.

October 3

There are three of us. The Lord comes and sits down alongside us. He really is seated, just like us, but perhaps a little more collected.

I feel you so incredibly present next to us, next to me, Lord.

✝ *I am here to pray to the Father with you and like you.*

You are at one and the same time incredibly real and light.

✝ *Do not make any plans or projects. Let me do things and act for you. I am the one who is leading this Community.*

October 4

✠ *Do not dream about the impossible. Do what is possible.*

This word of the Lord touches a friend who came for Mass and to whom Pierre, just a few moments earlier, had said almost the same thing.

October 5

Pierre and I were asked to come and speak about the *Compagnons du Partage.*

I'm delighted to have an audience again, and this time I'm not trying to get them to love the English language, but Jesus. In a way, it's easier. I have a general outline in my head, which Philippe prepared for me so I wouldn't go running off in all directions, and with it I try to speak calmly and simply about our life with the Companions. It flows easily; afterward a lot of people come to ask me questions and, above all, to tell me that they sensed my faith in the God-man who inspires us.

A little voice tells me:

✝ *I will make you a queen. Just as I told you.*

An older man who's a little intimidating comes up to thank me. He tells me he's taking away just one thought from the whole day. I ask him what it is. He rummages through his papers and reads it. Someone had asked me what our success rate was over the past four years, and I had answered:

"If you want a number, put down that maybe we 're-arrange' 10 percent. Whatever efficacy we have or results we have achieved belong to the invisible kingdom."

I feel proud and happy to have passed on the message. Not conceited, but proud to have been a good instrument, a good servant that day.

I almost forgot . . . Another gentleman came running up to me just as I was leaving and demanded to know where my husband was.

"He's not here."

"What a shame."

"Why do you say that?"

"I would have loved to meet this man. He must be a saint."

A little dumbfounded, I ask him:

"Why do you think that?"

"Well, you must often have to spend six to eight hours a day with the Companions. But you tell us that your kids are fine. So your husband must be a saint."

Cherchez la femme? Not at all. *Cherchez le roi*—Look for the king. Philippe will enter the kingdom before me!

October 13

Pierre concelebrates with Jean-Marc, the Abbot of Tamié. The congregation is just me. There is a sense of harmony right from the start. The Lord is standing, smiling, rejoicing over this complicity in the act of giving praise.

✞ *Come. Ask. I am an inexhaustible treasure.*
Dig in, not just with your hands, but up to
your elbows.

Pierre asks the Lord why so few of the Companions know him.

✞ *Do not worry about it. I am among them.*

October 15

Hubert, Isidore, and two Companions.

We didn't close the circle. The Lord comes and takes the empty space, sitting down on the floor!

Why are you sitting on the floor?

✝ *I am the bond. I come to unite. I place myself where there is room. Leave me some room in your hearts. I put myself where you need me, where there is division and pain. Make room for me.*

October 16

We feel very close.

Laurette:

"Mom, I went to Mass at the Carmel with Dad yesterday, and I realized how much I like to go with him. But I'm not sure whether I have any faith."

"Why do you say that?"

"What if Jesus' friends, the apostles, were mistaken? What if Jesus never existed?"

"But he did exist. Leave the door of your heart open to him. Then he'll be able to come in and live in your house."

"I know what you're talking about. You and Dad have a lot of influence on me. I go to Mass because you go, but it's not the same for me."

"What do you mean?"

"When you pray, I can see that you really believe he exists."

October 16

I'm overcome by a profound drowsiness. I feel like lying down. I feel so peaceful. It's all I can do not to stretch out on the carpet.

Thank you. Thank you.

✠ *This is the circle of my glory. Many have already entered into it. You are a part of it. Be happy and joyful.*

A little later I say to him:

It's difficult to hoist others up to you. It's a heavy task.

✠ *Be like the yeast in the dough. Be little. Do not worry about whether the dough is rising.*

October 17

✝ *Do not be afraid. I will lead you to the other shore. You are on the open sea. You can no longer see the shore you have left, nor can you see the one I am leading you toward.*

We are on the open sea, Lord. Sometimes I get seasick.

✝ *Do not be afraid. I am at the helm of the boat.*

October 18

It's hard for me to forget mundane things. Silly and worldly ideas weigh me down. I tell him so.

> Lord, it's hard-going today.

And later:

> What we do for the poor you give us, for the Companions, is make them a little less poor. But when we do that, you make us a little richer with yourself. Is that it?
>
> ✝ *Yes.*

October

It's the anniversary of the death of my friend Marcelle. Jesus is here in front of us along with Marcelle. Her head is slightly inclined. They're smiling.

I'm flabbergasted.

> Why are you doing this, Lord?

> ✝ *So that you may believe. Do you believe that she is really alive?*

Yes.

My *yes* is a little timid.

> ✝ *Believe.*

Later he says to me:

> ✝ *Look at her. Remember. I answered your prayer.*

And it's true.

> Lord, at least we're on the right road. We believe in you.

> ✝ *Yes, you do. But you can do still more.*

Just what the teacher used to write on our assignments: "Can be improved."

Two days before her death, Marcelle asked me if she was going to die. When I said yes, she used an emaciated finger to write in the air, "It's hard." And then she added, "You are strong."

"We're talking about your death, Marcelle, not mine," I replied. In a certain sense, the death of others is always easier to deal with.

We cried, and then we prayed together, and when it seemed that she was a little more calm, I entrusted two things to her. It was like a cry that came from the depths of my being.

Marcelle, I entrust my family to you, and the Community as well. Take them with you. I give them to you. Don't forget them.

She nodded yes, twice.

> Yes, Lord. I know that you took care of all this, that you answered my prayers, even though I did nothing to deserve it. One by one, the difficulties we were facing in the Community were smoothed out. The person who wanted to take over the direction of the Community backed off and stopped attacking us. The volunteers and hired staff who joined us for the purpose of working out their own problems have left. And those who were power hungry, jealous, and spiteful went away on their own. And just as I

was on the verge of giving up, having already lost about fifteen pounds, Pierre arrived on the scene. That very day I knew we were saved. I knew it in the very depths of my being when Pierre decided, right after arriving, to keep your real presence here. I was convinced the most difficult times were behind us. Critical and skeptical friends, whose comments were sometimes very painful, stopped their attacks because we had become credible in the eyes of the city. No longer did I have to listen to "Who's looking after the children?" and "Don't forget to take care of yourself," "Don't overdo it," "Don't try to pretend you're one of the poor," . . .

There are still some who don't understand and are waiting for me to start teaching or giving lectures again. It took the presence of the bishop, the wife of the governor of the Eure-et-Loire Department, and members of the Departmental council from both the right and the left of the political spectrum at our annual board meeting to make us (or was it just me?) feel that we had finally arrived. Yes, Lord, this is all true. You were with us. Yes, I do believe.

Today the Lord seems to be asking me, asking us, that this moment not be just a moment, but that it last.

October 23

As I walk to the Community we speak to each other.

Lord, what we are doing for the poor is a mere trifle. What it comes down to at times is little more than a smile or a handshake. That's not very much.

✝ *You misunderstand.*

What do you mean?

✝ *Be intense and light.*

Intense?

✝ *Intense in my relationship with you. Live it out intensely. But be light as well, because it is not you who are doing these things; it is I.*

In the evening, at Mass in the Hermitage, the Lord comes and takes me in his arms. It's as if I'm wrapped in a thick layer of tenderness. I'm overwhelmed by peace, a sense of presence, and pure love.

Why all this, Lord?

✝ *So that you may never turn away from me or allow yourself to be turned away.*

Yesterday I drove with a friend to a funeral, and for almost five hours we talked about death and about Jesus. He lost his wife two years ago and he's still rebelling against it. I try to tell him about my experience, but it's difficult. His anguish, his honesty, and his rebellion touch me and leave me disabled, a little wounded.

Today it seems that the Lord wants to remind me that it's not up to me to convert people. I'm to stay small, mute at times, but still be present to the suffering of others. If Jesus wants to make the dough rise, he'll do it in his own way.

October 24

There are several of us. The Lord comes and sits down beside us. His white robe extends to his feet. I'm intrigued by this long full robe or coat. I tell him so.

Why are you wearing this?

As so often happens, his reply comes after the Consecration.

✣ *Nicole, do you see how loosely this garment I am wearing fits me? It is very ample. I will clothe you with this garment. When you move around, when you walk, you will feel it on you, brushing against your limbs.*

What do you want to tell us?

✣ *That I move around and that I am alive. You wear me and I am with you.*

October 27

Vacation—just me and five kids. The sea is gentle. Our house on the sea is bathed in sunlight. The children are happy and relaxed.

The church where we go for Mass is ugly but full. The celebration is lively and the five children are insufferably cute as they make faces and comment on what is going on. I'm happy to be with them.

Fishnets are suspended from the vaulting of the nave. A large crucifix dominates the church.

I speak to him:

> Lord, why are there so few people who accept
> you, so few who take advantage of the abundant
> life that you offer us? All those others, why
> don't they come to you?

> ✝ *I am alive, Nicole. I am not an abstract idea*
> *or a system, but a living person. In order to*
> *know me and live with me, you have to*
> *choose me, to want me.*

Is it a little like choosing a traveling companion?

✝ *Yes. In order to know my light, you have to enter into a relationship with me. It takes two.*

October 29

Chapters 13 and 17 of the Gospel of John.

As I read these words and live these moments with Jesus, I feel like I'm one of the family. It's hard to write this lest I turn out to be vain or puffed up with pride. In fact, it's infinitely more simple: I know that I am one of his family, one of his friends. I believe that he had to die in order for me to receive the Holy Spirit so that he could live in me. I understand, not just intellectually, but with my whole being, that he had to die. It's absolutely clear to me. Yes, I believe in this man.

I leave the children for a few minutes as they're playing on the rocks and go back to rejoin him in the Batz church. Filled with the memory of the moments I have just relived, I let myself sink into him for a moment.

Then we speak to each other.

> Lord, I know that I'm yours, but I'm still a little afraid.

He knows that I'm afraid, and he knows why. Still, I tell him.

> There will be persecutions. You told me so. You told all of us. You also know, Lord, that I need

to be with the world. Ever since I began follow-
ing you more closely, especially in the company
of the Community, you know that there is sometimes a kind of separation between me after
being reborn in you and other people. It scares
me a little.

✝ *Do not be afraid. These are nothing but little
scratches.*

The word *scratches* comes back to me very strongly. I hang
on to it even though I don't understand it very well.

As I'm leaving the church, Jesus patiently explains it to me.

✝ *When you were little, you took your father's
hand, remember? You loved to do it. He reassured you, but still you were a little afraid.*

Yes, I do remember. In fact, I remember something very specific. Once, when we were living
in Austria, my father killed a crow—or something that looked like a crow—and he made me
pick it up in order to show me that this ugly
beast was harmless. I was afraid to pick it up, so
I kept holding on to his hand.

✝ *Your father let go of your hand. That is nor-
mal. But now I am holding your hand, as
your father did.*

Lord, you know that I want to show him my
notebook. I have wanted to for quite a while.
You also know why. May I?

✝ *Yes, you may.*

Once again I weep, gently and without sadness.

November

In church a lot of people and a lot of singing. Almost too much. It gets in the way. It's hard to encounter him if there isn't any peace and quiet.

His face looms over me. Large, huge. He takes up all the space between the floor and the ceiling of the nave.

> Why are you showing me your face? And why is it so large?

After the Consecration he replies:

> ✝ *Because I am alive. I have a face, Nicole, and like all faces, it is animated, expressive; it lives.*

You mean you smile, you weep, you're sad . . .

> ✝ *Yes. I am alive.*

November 4

Another planet. I'm back at the Community. Everything is whizzing by at a hundred miles an hour. It's not easy to keep up. I'm trying. We have a new director who used to be at an orphanage in Auteuil. The Lord is keeping his promise to make the Community grow. That's what he's doing. I'm happy at heart, even if things are happening so fast here with the Companions that I can't keep up.

At Mass I see the image of a man who is standing and loaded down with packages. They're all over the place.

> You see, Lord. It's hard to have to carry so
> much.

> ✝ *Yes. It is hard if you think that you are the*
> *only one who is doing the carrying. Believe*
> *that I am carrying, too, helping you carry. I*
> *carry the heaviest things. I help you.*

November 5

There are a lot of us. Some Companions are in front of me. They sit there, stooped over, their hands all muddy, and not exactly smelling of Chanel No. Five. Those assigned to read the lessons stumble through them. My heart is touched at the sight of such poverty, and yet I can't keep myself from asking him:

> Are they really the people you prefer? Why is that?

> ✝ *They have not built up any fortresses, any barricades around themselves. They have not used their intelligence to construct a system against me.*

As I walk toward the Community, I reflect on some phrases from the Gospel:

> Lord, it's strange that you should say this to us. I believe that everything—friendship, love—is based on mutuality. I'm not talking about giving for the sake of getting something back, but still, you can't just give or just receive.

> ✝ *You are right, Nicole. When you give something to a poor person who is unable to repay you, I will repay you, because you gave it to me.*

November 7

There are quite a few of us. Companions and some friends. The Lord comes to tell us:

> ☩ *Do not be afraid. In your shortsightedness,*
> *you let yourselves be weighed down by all*
> *you have to do, by your cares and problems,*
> *by tomorrow and yesterday. Do not be afraid.*
> *You have to go beyond all that. I can see far-*
> *ther than you. I know.*

From the beginning of Mass, Jesus, who is seated alongside me, has held me to his heart. I felt good leaning against him, but sad at the same time, since I felt myself weighed down by all my responsibilities at home and elsewhere and by the fact that Pierre is going to be leaving soon to preach a retreat. Without him around it's hard to manage, but I'm happy that he's going to do what he's made for, namely to speak about his relationship with the Jesus he follows.

> And that's why you're holding me so close to
> you, Lord. You know all this.

> ☩ *Yes, I do. Do not be afraid. I am alive. I want*
> *you to sense it, and that is why I am holding*
> *you so close to me.*

November 10

Jesus kneels and holds my face in his hands.

Why are you doing this, Lord?

✝ *I want you to sense that I am alive. Give me the gift of believing that I am alive, that I protect you and go before you.*

Tomorrow Pierre is going away and leaving me at the helm of this double community, the Hermitage and the center here in town. I already know that it's not going to be easy.

November 12

As I expected, Pierre is hardly gone and he has left a storm behind him and a great void.

The storm erupts over the rivalry between two staff members. All hell breaks loose. The three of us get together and put our cards on the table. I listen. One is angry, the other hurt. I'm calm inside. I intervene very little, but I do so firmly. I remind them that we are here to work together. The storm abates. One of them asks the other for pardon. My heart leaps for joy. A few minutes later we take Communion together with some Companions. I can't get over the sense of peace! It was a true gift. The hands holding my face were truly his.

November 13

It's Wednesday today, and that means my little family gets to monopolize its mother. Nothing unusual about that. The friend of an Orthodox friend of mine drops in for a few minutes. Her intelligence and, above all, her spirituality bring a warm glow to the house and to some guests of ours. And then I have to run off to the Companions. When I arrive I'm a little out of breath. One of the Companions is there.

"We were waiting for you. Are you going to say the Mass?"

"No, Jean-Pierre."

I explain that what we had yesterday was a Communion service, and that today and hereafter, while Pierre is away, we will have a half-hour period of Adoration.

"No problem," he says. "It's all the same to me."

And so all four of us remained there, three Companions and I, before the Lord in silence. The silence was real. Such a gift. I thank the Lord.

✝ *I will make you a queen.*

And then a few moments later:

> ✝ *Take me into yourself. Let me fill all the space within you.*

His hands touch my face. Of course I say yes. How could I refuse?

> I don't deserve any of this, Lord. I feel completely satisfied and still surprised. What do you want to do in me?

> ✝ *I want to expand in you.*

And me? What am I to do?

> ✝ *Enter into yourself to ask me what you should do. Question me within yourself. Do not act, do not reflect from the outside. Enter into yourself to question me.*

The Lord is unbelievable!

This evening I asked him to send workers into the harvest, to enlarge our Community and establish it in the city.

> There is too much misery in the streets. Please do something, Lord.

November 14

✝ *I am here. Let me work through you.*

What do you mean?

✝ *Within this Community and for this Community, act and live as if you were expecting everything from me. Do not plan anything, except what depends on you.*

But, Lord, we have some situations here that are not very easy to deal with. You know that better than I.

✝ *I will answer you; I will tell you what you should say at the time you need it. Do not worry about anything.*

November 15

A full day, but a peaceful one. At the Hermitage the entire team is working. Ernest, the new associate director, and I are given a warm welcome. The work is going ahead very well. I thank the Lord for all these smiling faces and for the proposals we have talked about.

Pierre isn't here this evening. Every Friday he speaks to them about this man Jesus. I'll have to take his place. On my knees in the chapel I tell the Lord about my fear.

> I'm too intellectual for them, Lord. Help me to
> speak of you.

I open the Bible and the passage given me is the one about Mary Magdalene with the gardener in front of the stone that has been rolled away. I speak. It's relatively easy. I feel like Mary Magdalene, amazed at such love, such sensitivity and tenderness.

A few minutes later, I'm in the chapel for a period of Adoration.

> ✝ *I will make this Community grow. Do not ask*
> *me where, when, or how. I will do it.*

What about me, Lord? What am I to do?

✝ *You are letting me work through you. And I will.*

November 17

I speak to him before going to Mass and at the beginning of the Mass.

> Lord, one of my relatives is mean and belligerent. She's having a hard time, Lord. And the 23,000 people who were killed when that volcano erupted in Colombia. It's just dreadful, Lord.

> ✝ *Yes, I know.*

> Say something. Speak to me.

> ✝ *If your relative is feeling depressed or a catastrophe happens at the other end of the world, there is really nothing you can do. It is beyond you. You are not able to do anything about it. So let it go.*

> But if I let it go, that means I'm running away from it. It's like saying, "Since it's not my fault, I can forget about it."

> ✝ *No, you are not running away. You are being like me. You are sharing the suffering, and you are praying.*

I'm sorry, but to me that sounds like running away.

✝ *No. Do what depends on you.*

What is that?

✝ *Pray and give me shelter.*

You want to take shelter in me?

✝ *Yes, I want to stay with you, live in you.*

Why?

✝ *To do what you cannot do by yourself. I will do it. I am the only one who can do it.*

Yes, I do understand what the Lord wants to tell me. He will do what I can't do, provided I give him space.

> I think I understand what you want to tell me. But why do you want to come and stay with me? It's not always very nice in here. I'm really amazed that you'd choose me as a place to do the work of building your kingdom.
>
> ✝ *But why not, Nicole? After all, I was born in a barn.*
>
> Amen, Lord. And even though I'm usually so sensitive, I'm not at all miffed to learn that I'm not a five-star hotel! Move in. I will proclaim your marvels.

November 18

There are five of us: Ernest, who is our new associate director, and three Companions. Jesus is here.

> Thank you, Lord, for everything you're giving this Community. I marvel a bit that Ernest and the Companions are here.

> ✝ *Did I not tell you? Did I not promise you? I will do even more. Let me walk ahead of you more.*

> Thank you, Lord. It's true that I'm now putting you on right-side out. Am I wearing you correctly now?

> ✝ *Yes.*

> And you want this clothing to keep me warm so that I really feel you?

> ✝ *Yes.*

> And that's why you're spoiling me so much?

> ✝ *Yes.*

November 19

A busy day at home and a lot of activity at the Community. Two contentious hoodlums show up, and it's hard for me to stay calm. A eucharistic service this evening in the chapel. We had been using a construction shed for a chapel, but now we need it to house two men. Delicately, we move the Blessed Sacrament (the Lord) to a smaller hut. Only half of it has been cleaned. We follow him and place him in the clean part. Our shared conversation is impressive. One of the Companions tells us about his suffering. It's very moving. The Lord speaks to us.

> ✢ *Be really united among yourselves. I am the bond between you. Brothers and sisters. Do not be afraid.*

This evening, prayer with the *Bon Secours* sisters. There are ten of us, including a priest. The Lord speaks a lot and uses me a lot, as well. I used to be afraid to lead prayer in the presence of all these professionals, but now I not only feel confident, but peaceful.

November 20

There are five of us.

✢ *I will increase this Community. I will continue
to act. Do not be afraid.*

I believe you, Lord, and I'm not even concerned
to know where, when, and with whom. I just
believe you will do it. I'm going to try to leave
you the biggest place.

✢ *Yes. Do your work well. Do not worry. I will
do it with you.*

Greater things than I could do alone? Is that it?

✢ *Yes.*

I know why, Lord. Because I'm two. There are
two of us working for your kingdom. You have
passed through death, Lord, so that everyone
who believes in you may be two.

✢ *Yes.*

November 21

I look at his face. It's the same face as on the Holy Shroud.

Your death must have been dreadful, Lord—
such affliction, such anguish.

✝ *Yes.*

Even with your Father who loved you and
whom you loved, it was dreadful.

✝ *Yes, but it had to be. And now you also know
that you have to pass through death in order
to find hope. I had to give you that hope.*

Yes, Jesus. It's truly a cross. But now you can
act in us and with us because you have been
victorious once and for all.

✝ *Yes.*

But how they have disfigured your cross and
your message, Lord.

✝ *Yes.*

November 22

✢ *Do not be afraid. I will do it for you, for all of you, for this Community.*

I'm reassured as he touches my face with his hands.

November 23

It was a difficult day. One of the Companions who used to pray with us regularly started drinking again and has become miserable and aggressive.

It's tough. His anguish is more painful to me than his hostility. Our future associate director is present, close by. He lets himself be struck and says nothing. The Companion leaves. I cry.

> He's so miserable, Lord.

> ✝ *Yes, I know.*

> Talk to me.

> ✝ *You know how I feel every time you turn your backs on me and refuse me. You know. His anguish is the same as mine. I am part of it, Nicole.*

> Lord, you force me to look at myself, my own failings, my own turning away, and yet you tell me that you're ready to take me back in your arms again. Is that right?

> ✝ *Yes.*

November 24

Two staff, four Companions. I divide the Host. Jesus is here, minuscule but living.

> Tell me, Lord, what is the link between human distress and your own love? How far apart are they?

> ✝ *I will take you from floor to floor. Do not stay on the ground floor. Do not be content with a shortsighted view. The house that I am giving you to live in has several stories. Do not be satisfied with the basement.*

> Will you show me the other levels?

> ✝ *Yes.*

November 28

Pierre is back. With him present, I can handle anything with the Companions. The burden is infinitely lighter. There is a song in my heart, and the sadness of the past three days gives way to happiness.

I'm happy, Jesus.

✝ *Yes, I know. I am sharing it.*

You really are alive.

✝ *Yes. Yesterday you and I shared your sorrow. Today I am rejoicing with you.*

And then, after praying in tongues:

✝ *Do not press me. I will take care of it. I will enlarge the Community. Do not be afraid.*

November

After the Consecration:

> Where do I live in this house you have spoken
> about, Lord?

> ✠ *You live on the first floor. But really live in it.*
> *You have things to do. Do them well.*

> You mean my daily tasks, the nuisances, deci-
> sions, telephone calls, projects?

> ✠ *Yes. Do them well.*

> Who lives on the second floor?

> ✠ *Those you hear walking overhead, over your*
> *heart sometimes. Those who press you, who*
> *get in your way every now and then.*

> What should I do about them?

> ✠ *Listen to them, Nicole. Listen to the sounds*
> *they make. Do not seal yourself off from them.*

> What do you mean by that?

✝ *You do not have to move in with them or live with them. Live on your own floor, but listen to the sounds they make. Do not forget them.*

November

Lord, I have to love and help those who live above me. Both of us have to listen to them.

✝ *Yes.*

But without wanting to do everything for them or live with them, right?

✝ *Yes.*

And above them, Jesus? Who lives above them?

✝ *Those whom I have in reserve to help you, to love you, to guide you.*

Do I know them?

✝ *No, not all of them. But I know them and I am preparing them for you, for the others, and for the Community.*

In fact, the Lord has always provided me with hands and hearts when things became too difficult, when I had to undertake a new venture or overcome difficulties.

Thank you.

November

There are about twenty of us. We pray for those who have
died and in whose memory we have come together today.

After the Consecration:

> Who lives on the top floor?
>
> ✝ *The multitude of those who are already with
> me and who are ready to help you.*
>
> Marie, Etienne, Philippe's parents, and so many
> others. I call on them.
>
> ✝ *They are not that far away. They are among
> the living, Nicole. You have to believe that.*

A little later:

> We don't go to you all by ourselves, Lord. We
> have to go to you with the whole house, with all
> the floors of it.
>
> ✝ *Yes.*

December 3

A marvelous respite with the Lord after a pretty exhausting day. Shopping and housecleaning in the morning, lunch with a friend who is suffering from depression, monthly conferences with each of the Companions.

I'm heartened by this peace that draws me into the Lord.

> Thank you, Lord. I'm always surprised and amazed that you choose to come and live in me.

> ✝ *Do a good job of getting the straw ready for me. That is all I need. Something simple. Do not welcome me with too many decorations and trimmings. Just your heart.*

December 6

The cathedral is full of children and Marist priests who have come together for a traditional Marian celebration. I feel a little out of place in this community. A simple and prayerful tone is set right at the beginning of the celebration. The Gospel of the angel telling Mary that she will be a mother makes my heart leap. Almost every word affects me as if I were Mary and as if the angel were speaking to me. I try to pull myself together, but don't succeed. I feel as if I'm sinking, drowning. I'm not going to pretend that I'm the Virgin Mary. Am I going crazy? The experience is so strong that I'm not able to hold back my tears as I undergo it.

And then Mary comes toward me. She's dressed in blue, accompanied by her Son. She points to him and humbly tells me:

He needs you. My Son needs you.

This is way too much for me. I feel that I'm foundering, and in a panic I ask Jesus:

Speak to me. Give me a sign. Show me that I'm not dreaming, that I'm not going crazy.

The priest gets up to give the sermon. He's a simple man, and everyone appears to love him, especially the children.

"At this moment, the Lord is speaking to your hearts. He's asking you to follow him. Listen to him."

His sermon is a love poem, a love poem winging up to God.

I'm not crazy. Jesus wants me to be his servant. He wants Mary's *yes*. He wants me to be like Mary.

> Lord, look at me. Look at my limitations, look at what you're asking of me. You want us to expand the Community, but there are so few of us. It's a heavy load for Pierre and me. And yet you want us to expand?
>
> ✝ *Yes.*

A little later I said yes. It was the humble *yes* of a servant. All I'm sure of is my good will.

So be it.

December 12–15

Things are happening fast. At home, with the Companions. The two planets on which I live are hard to handle. Philippe has been exhausted for the past two weeks; the kids are on edge with the approach of Christmas; a friend criticizes me harshly for being too liberal; I have to take charge of the annual board meeting . . . It's way too much. I'm doing my best to live in the present moment. But it's very difficult for me truly to be present on these two planets that are so different from each other. A minitempest hits, in me first, and then with a friend. Everything seems to be intent on upsetting my equilibrium.

Mass at the chapel: a moment of peace.

> ✝ *The sea is rough, Nicole. I am here.*

Where, Lord?

> ✝ *Look at me. I am the rope that you see. Be the buoy in the sea.*

The image is that of a storm-tossed sea with a buoy bobbing to and fro. The buoy is me.

Why, Lord?

✝ *That is how I want you. I want others to see you.*

And what's to become of me?

✝ *You will hold on to me.*

Where are you?

✝ *The rope that comes down from the sky and secures the buoy. Hold on to me.*

The storm didn't let up. It lasted through a whole sleepless night of intense struggle.

Calm was finally restored the next evening. I have the impression that evil forces were making sport of me and using me as a plaything.

Why, Lord? You know how hard I fought. Why?

✝ *You were not fastened to the rope—to me— tight enough. You knew it was there, but you really did not come and hold on to it.*

I think about it, and he's right.

Next time I'll try, Lord. I promise you. I'll try harder.

He smiles.

I'm completely beat. I'll sleep soundly tonight.

December 16
and following

Full days. Pierre is worn out. Another bout of multiple sclerosis. He only hears in one ear. He still has a smile and a kind word for everyone, but I feel sorry for him. Philippe is also beat. He's had a battery of tests. Nothing serious, but every now and then he gets run down. Laurette is sick, and though it's not serious, she has to spend two days in bed. In the middle of all this I keep on going, happy to get gifts ready for the family and all the Companions. Taking care of a thousand and one details and being on hand for everybody leaves me completely exhausted when evening rolls around. And yet the Lord wants us to expand!

> You know all this, Lord. Are you sure about what you're telling us?
>
> ✝ *Yes.*
>
> Look at my limitations. Look at what you're asking of me.
>
> ✝ *Nicole, I will carry you. I will carry you like a babe in my arms. Let go.*
>
> What about Pierre?

✢ *I am holding him to my heart. Do not be afraid. I have him tightly in my arms.*

December

The next day at the Chapel of the Companions, Mass:

✝ *Have faith. All of you, have faith. Be like me.*

It's hard.

✝ *Nicole, I was born in a stable and died on a cross. What more do you want? What greater proof of my love do you need? Nicole, I need your trust. I need you to be like a little servant. I will make you a queen, Nicole. I am already doing it.*

You're right, Lord. I can tell. But are you really asking me to do nothing? Do you simply want us to let ourselves be carried by you?

✝ *Yes.*

What about all the others?

✝ *They will look at you and all the rest, and they will follow us. When they see us—Pierre and me, you and me, the Community and me—they will come to me.*

December 24

All sorts of last-minute shopping to take care of with Laurette sick in bed. This evening we are going to join my family in Rambouillet. Before leaving, I drop in at the hall where the *Secours Catholique* is hosting a meal for more than three hundred people. The poor are there. We say hello. We know one another. As I'm leaving I see someone silhouetted in the dark coming toward the door. I feel uneasy. At the last minute I recognize Jean-Luc. He's drunk and there is hatred in his eyes. I leave; the family is waiting for me. Later on I find out that he got into a fight with the director of the *Secours Catholique* and that the demonic force in him was so strong it took four people to subdue him. Pierre came and prayed, and Jean-Luc immediately calmed down and began to cry. The demons left him, for the time being at least.

Christmas with my family was calm and peaceful. At the Companions there were eighteen for Mass, and when we gave presents the next day, there was a look of tenderness in the eyes of those broken men.

End of December, beginning of January

There's so much to do. In the evening I am too tired to write. I need peace and quiet to write down what he tells us.

It's heavy-going right now. The tribe is tired, on edge. The little patience I have gets used up quickly by the care I have to take not to step on anyone's toes. I'm afraid that I'm not keeping my priorities in order. I'm worried about the future of the Community, and I tell him so.

> ✝ *Do not be afraid. The preparations for your party have already been taken care of. I have already set the table.*

I see an immense white tablecloth.

> Why this image, Lord?

> ✝ *So that you may sense deep inside that I am already waiting for you. Do not be afraid.*

The next day the image is sharper. My table is set and I feel deep down that Jesus wants to tell me that his kingdom has already begun here below, that I don't have anything to fear.

The next day he receives me with wide-open arms. A light so strong that it's almost blinding seems to radiate from them. I draw near, but the light is so strong that I can't enter into it completely.

✝ *It is too soon. It is too strong for you. Wait. You will see.*

Something incredible happens the next day. After the Consecration, a light settles on my face. It seems as if I'm illuminated, bathed in immense softness. And I hear these unbelievable words:

✝ *You are beautiful. I love you like this.*

I have to say it again: it's unbelievable.

(By the way, I forgot to say that one of the Companions, whom I trusted, has taken off with my car, my papers, etc. I keep my calm. This isn't the first time one of them has betrayed our confidence, nor will it be the last. I find this theft infinitely easier to take than the insults or the hatred of some of the others.)

And then, on Sunday, water damage in the house. The library got it. My favorite room. The ceiling has to be repaired, the books are ruined . . . I have a good cry. I guess I'm not as unattached as I thought!

January 9

We pray for those who are absent, for my thief, for those who have left us. We are at peace.

After the Consecration, the Lord says to us:

✝ *Do not be upset. Let me get into your boat. I will guide it. Let me get in and you will not be afraid of anything.*

The sea is always rough, Lord.

✝ *Yes, but with me in your boat, you do not have to be afraid of anything. I will be here with you in the storm. I will protect you.*

January 10

✝ *Make the most of the moment I give you.*
Do not sell the present short. Live fully in
the here and now; I will take care of tomor-
row. Do not let yourself be weighed down by
worrying about the future. I will act.

All these days in January have been difficult, so harried
that I haven't even been able to write every evening. First
of all, there's Philippe, who is worn out and ill. It's been
dragging on for a month. Ever since the beginning of
January I feel I've been pulled in all directions for the sake
of the Community. I feel that I'm being used for everything
and for nothing. It's difficult and I'm tired.

This evening my heart is in turmoil. Philippe is completely
spent. I'm anxious about his sunken appearance. I'm not
going to Algeria to hike on the Ahaggar plateau, even
though it's a respite that I was so looking forward to. Benoît
is a full-fledged teenager and rejects his mother: nothing
unusual about that, but still difficult for me to accept.

Mass at the Hermitage. I try not to cry, but I can't take it
anymore.

> Lord, I'm on my knees. I've had it. Surely you
> see how heavy my burden is.

✝ *Yes, I know.*

And then, without speaking, he comes toward me and stretches out his arms to me.

✝ *Do not be upset. I know. I am going to help you.*

The next day I feel a little better, but I still have a hard time making any headway.

✝ *I am helping you walk. I am beside you.*

The evening is pure anguish. After getting inconclusive results on a blood test, I wait for two hours for the doctor's verdict. All I can do is wait. Minute by minute, I get on with what I have to do. The children, supper, the telephone . . . The doctor says there is nothing to worry about, and Laurette is surprised at how calm I was. My heart beat wildly, but I was being helped.

January 19

✝ *I grasp you by the shoulders. I am your companion. I am really here.*

Why is that, Lord?

✝ *You need it. You need to feel my tenderness and my love for you.*

This evening at Mass his presence was so overpowering that I almost collapsed.

January 20–22

✝ *Rejoice to have me for your shepherd. Be happy.*

✝ *Say* yes *to me. Not* yes but, *but* YES. *A real* yes.

✝ *Be like David. Fight with the arms that I give you, with what you are. Do not look for any other protection but me. I will help you.*

January 23 and following

The sea is storm tossed. Philippe needs to be hospitalized for a week. We have to find a place in Paris. I feel bad for him, and of course I'm worried, but I'm not distraught. I'm determined to live in the present, and I'm managing to do that because I really feel that I'm being helped. I'm sleeping normally and trying to do well what needs to be done. Jesus accompanies me, attentive and kind. I sense him at the Eucharist, of course, but also in the calm I feel in spite of myself. He knows what he's doing. And so I hold his hand firmly.

On January 25 after the Eucharist, his face is next to mine. I'm infused with an ineffable sweetness and tenderness. His face is like a beam of light that goes through every part of me, leaving me in great peace.

Do you have something to tell me?

✝ *I am here. I want you to feel me. I am living in you, around you, through you.*

Thank you.

January 27

The Lord asks us to bring him our gifts, like the three kings.

> What gifts are you talking about, Jesus? I'm not
> rich, nor is the Community.

> ✝ *Bring me what you are.*

I give him these difficult days, these comings and goings
between the Community, home, the drugstore, and the lab
to get the results of Philippe's tests . . . to say nothing of the
endless shopping trips to make sure that the family has
some food on the table every day.

He accepts it all. I'm sure of it.

January 28

✝ *Stretch yourself out on my tenderness, on my love. I love you. That is understood.*

January 30

✝ *Look at me. Look at my face. I know that the road is rocky. Do not look down at your feet. I am a companion. I walk ahead of you, but I slow down in order to walk with you. Follow me. I am the road.*